T0208308

In the Hollow of His Hand

IN THE HOLLOW OF HIS HAND

Amazing Stories of God's Care

GORMAN ✦ WOODFIN

MULTNOMAH
BOOKS

IN THE HOLLOW OF HIS HAND
published by Multnomah Books

© 2001 by Gorman Woodfin

International Standard Book Number: 978-1-59052-814-3

Cover image of person by Tony Stone Images
Background cover image by Scott Goff/Index Stock Imagery
Photo of the author taken by Jim Anklam

Published in the United States by WaterBrook Multnomah, an imprint of
the Crown Publishing Group, a division of Random House Inc., New York.

MULTNOMAH and its mountain colophon are registered trademarks
of Random House Inc.

ALL RIGHTS RESERVED
No part of this publication may be reproduced, stored in a retrieval system,
or transmitted, in any form or by any means—electronic, mechanical,
photocopying, recording, or otherwise—without prior written permission.

For information:
MULTNOMAH BOOKS
12265 Oracle Boulevard, Suite 200
Colorado Springs, CO 80921

Library of Congress Cataloging-in-Publication Data:
Woodfin, Gorman.
   In the hollow of His hand / by Gorman Woodfin.
      p. cm.
      ISBN 9781590528143 (pbk.)
   1. Christian biography. I. Title.
   BR1700.2 .W68 2001
      270'.092'2—dc21
         2001003173

146651086

"Captivating stories of God's awesome, delivering power in the lives of everyday people!"

BYRON JONES, VICE PRESIDENT OF ENTERTAINMENT
CLOUD TEN PICTURES

"These real-life stories are an inspiration, showing how God's love for us always prevails."

PETER LALONDE, CEO, CLOUD TEN PICTURES

"In one of the great hymns of the church, we sing 'Grant us wisdom; grant us courage.' This book shows the power and majesty of God's grace to grant wisdom and courage in the lives of some who have faced great trials. It should be in the library of every Christian."

DAVID GOODNOW, JOURNALIST AND
CNN INTERNATIONAL ANCHOR

"It is such an encouragement to see the hand of God take tragedy and loss and actually use it for our good. These stories are a strong reminder that 'If God is for us, who can be against us?'"

TERRY MEEUWSEN, COHOST OF *THE 700 CLUB*

"Gorman brings the same great ability evidenced in the countless stories he's produced for *The 700 Club* to his inspiring new book, *In the Hollow of His Hand*. These real-life dramatizations of God's power and grace will build your faith to say, 'If God can do *that* for them, maybe He can do *this* for me, too.'"

LISA RYAN, COHOST OF *THE 700 CLUB*

Dedication

I've always prayed that God would give me the right friends, those that would help me be closer to Him and the hollow of His hand.

First, to my family:
- To my older brothers, Woody and Randy, for their inspirational leadership.
- To my beautiful sister, Susan, for her love.
- To my dedicated mom and dad, who were willing to drive eight hours one way to watch me run around in tights and a doublet and perform Shakespeare.

Next, to my friends:
- To Jim, for his years of endless patience and encouragement.
- To Sharon, for her years of tireless support of my career.
- To my South Carolina support group, David and Charlotte, Viki and Becky B. Our years of laughter have meant the world to me.
- To my Tennessee supporters, Mark and Tracie (and Moose). Thanks for the refuge.

Last, to those that inspire:
- To all the amazing families involved in these stories.
- And to my new family at Multnomah Publishers.

Table of Contents

Introduction

Have you ever wondered if God has forsaken you? Be honest. Have you faced tragedy and bitter disappointment? Have you suffered the loss of a loved one? Perhaps you've been in the pit of despair. Perhaps you're still there now.

Has it ever made you wonder where God is in it all? Have you secretly questioned how a loving God could allow you to endure such calamity without intervening?

The people in this book have been there. They have suffered greatly—the loss of a child, the heartbreak of divorce, the darkness of drugs and vicious violence. More than most, they have earned the right to doubt God's love and care. Yet through it all they have come to realize that God was not only aware of their distress but also in it with them.

In the six years I have been a national reporter for the Christian Broadcasting Network, it has been my privilege to get to know these people and hear their stories. They aren't bedtime tales—some of them deal with addiction, murder, crime, and war. But in every one, I think you will see the amazing hand of God.

In the Old Testament, the children of Israel erected markers whenever God delivered them from an enemy or performed a miracle on their behalf. These piles of uncut stones became monuments of remembrance for God's people, prompting them to retell to their children the stories of His power and goodness.

My hope is that these stories will have the same effect in your life. I hope they will give you hope in your distress and remind you of God's care. In the words of Chip Gillette, the first officer on the scene of the Wedgwood Baptist Church shooting, "God is in control even in the midst of terror. Even when it looks like evil has triumphed, even in the midst of turmoil, God holds us in His hand."

You are about to take an incredible journey through pain and joy, failure and healing, horrible evil and unbelievable forgiveness. Yet through it all, you will see that God was holding these people in the hollow of His hand.

I think you'll find He's holding you, too.

KYLE JONES
When Lightning Strikes!

I saw Kyle's sneaker off to the side....
It was on fire and half-melted. His sock was disintegrated....
When the lightning exited his body, it basically
blew the sock and shoe right off his foot.

I t started out as a normal, peaceful Sunday. It was Mother's Day 1995. The Jones family of Sugarhill, Georgia, had gone to church that morning. Steven and Denise and their sons, Kyle, age ten, and Matthew, age eight, had settled into their Sunday afternoon routine.

Kyle and Matthew went up the street to play with some friends. Denise sat at her desk in front of an upstairs window doing some paperwork. Steven was down the hall vacuuming.

Just as Steven switched the vacuum off, they both heard the loudest crack of thunder they'd ever heard. Denise called down the hallway, "Wow, that was close!" They looked up at the sky. It wasn't stormy outside, just a bit cloudy. The lightning seemed to have come from nowhere. They had no concept that their lives were about to change forever with that single split second of electricity from the sky.

A minute after the crash, the phone rang. A neighbor frantically said, "Quick, Kyle's been hurt." Both Steven and Denise bolted for the door. Steven ran up the street. From the tone of the neighbor's voice, Denise thought that Kyle must have broken his leg and needed a doctor, so she went to get the car.

Steven raced up the hill in front of their home. He remembers the eerie feeling he had as he ran up to the wooded, vacant lot. "It was like running in slow motion. All the neighbors were standing there motionless, just watching me. I wondered why they were looking at me like that. Their faces were saying, 'He doesn't know what's happened. He doesn't know what he's about to see.'"

As Steven made it to his son's unconscious body, a haunting image forever burned itself in his brain. "When I first ran into the woods, I saw Kyle's sneaker off to the side about four or five feet away. It was on fire and half-melted. His sock was disintegrated. We believe the lightning went in through his hand and then came out his left foot. When the lightning exited his body, it basically blew the sock and shoe right off his foot."

Denise pulled up soon after. She rushed to Kyle and fell to her knees sobbing, "'Mommy's here.' I just wanted him to know I was there. His body was twisting so terribly."

"Kyle was basically lifeless," Steven says, "but his body was struggling to stay alive. I had never seen that before: someone just absolutely fighting to stay alive."

The neighbors were already helping their son. Two of them had begun CPR within critical minutes after Kyle's accident.

"We will never forget his eyes," Steven says. "They were a color you can't describe. They looked glazed and dead. It was unbelievable."

"They were like a cold gray with a small black dot for the pupil," Denise says.

The girl administering CPR did not realize who it was. She had been Kyle's baby-sitter, but she didn't recognize this boy with burns now disfiguring 70 percent of his body. Even his fingernails and toenails were melted.

"He had a combination of burns," Denise says. "Some were flash burns on the exterior, and some of them were like burning from the inside out. It was just incredible."

Kyle was rushed to a local hospital. His condition was so severe the medical personnel felt he should be transferred immediately to the regional burn unit at Grady Hospital in downtown Atlanta. Doctors had a difficult time getting a breathing tube down Kyle's throat. His chances of survival were minimal.

"There was a chaplain who came in and basically told us, 'Take a last look at your son,'" Denise says through tears. "He said, 'He's probably not going to make it to the burn center.'" So Steven and Denise slipped into Kyle's room and quietly looked at their son for what they thought might be the last time.

Miraculously, Kyle did make it to Grady Hospital. Steven rode to Atlanta in the ambulance with his son. Once in the emergency area, the boy was rushed into the ER.

Kyle's prognosis was awful. Nurses informed Steven and Denise of a formula used by doctors to determine the chances of survival for burn victims: You take the percentage of the body that is burned and add the age of the child. That is a rough calculation for the percentage of children who do not survive.

Steven and Denise added Kyle's ten years to the 70 percent of his body that was burned—giving him an 80 percent chance of not making it. And when the doctors added the damage caused by the electrocution, their conclusion was that there was little hope the boy would survive.

The medical staff immediately began pumping Kyle's body with massive amounts of fluids. With most of his skin burned away, his body could not hold the life-sustaining fluids that it desperately needed to survive.

But all through the nightmarish ordeal, Steven and Denise prayed for their son. From the very beginning, when they first ran up the street and saw Kyle's body smoldering from the lightning blast, they had been praying.

Since it was Sunday night, the Joneses' church quickly heard of Kyle's accident. A sign on the door of the church read, "The Sunday night service is canceled. Kyle Jones has been struck by lightning. Please pray."

Members of the small congregation made the trip to Atlanta to pray with Steven and Denise. Kyle's mom recalls that every time they looked up from their prayers she saw more people from church standing in the waiting room praying with them. Their regular Sunday night service had become a time of intense prayer for a defenseless boy fighting for his life.

Steven had called his parents as soon as he reached the hospital. He knew he had to talk to his father. "Dad always talked about walking daily with the Lord. I just wanted my dad interceding for Kyle the way Jesus intercedes for us."

Kyle miraculously made it through that first critical night. But it seemed as if he were only hanging on by a thread to his young life. Even his physical appearance began to change. Steven and Denise recall the deep pain they felt while watching their son suffer.

"He was swollen so much you really couldn't recognize him," Steven says. "I remember looking him over and trying to find one part of his body that I could say, 'That's my son.' And I couldn't do it."

His mom remembers, "His lips were so swollen around the air tube to his mouth that it looked like it was actually poked through his cheek." Denise also recalls the fluids they were pumping into Kyle's body. "It was gallons and gallons of fluids. And it just leaked out. He was on these pads that would absorb it. They were constantly changing those pads. They had to pump gallons of fluids into him so his kidneys wouldn't quit. It was awful."

Steven and Denise began to trade off shifts at the hospital. One of them needed to be at home with Matthew while the other kept vigil with Kyle. Denise knew that even if her son lived, his chances for a full recovery were about zero. She prayed as only a mother can: sad that her son was dying, broken that there was nothing she could do. But in her prayers, she asked God for a sign of hope. She desperately needed to know that her boy was going to be okay.

Early in the morning of the third day, Denise felt God give her a sign. "About two in the morning I was just praying with him and his eyes just opened a little bitty slit. He responded to everything I asked him. He nodded and he would mouth things. But they had a tube in his mouth so he couldn't speak.

"The first thing he mouthed was 'Matthew.' I told him that his brother was fine. I told Kyle he'd been hurt and asked if he remembered anything. He shook his head no. And I asked him if he was in pain. And he shook his head that he wasn't.

"He wanted to know where Dad was. I told him, 'He'll be in later.' I just told him he had been hurt and not to worry about anything." With tears welling up in her eyes, Denise remembers, "And I said, 'I love you. Go back to sleep.' And he mouthed, 'I love you, Mom.'

"And then I just knew—I knew he was going to be fine."

Denise was right: Her son was going to make it. But Kyle would face several serious medical procedures. With so much of his skin tissue destroyed, the doctors had to harvest healthy skin from Kyle's back to graft over the severely damaged areas of his body. After the operation, a plastic wrap was literally stapled around those areas to help hold the grafts in place and facilitate healing.

The young boy suffered through painful treatments that were necessary to help his body heal. Wraps extended over the entire length of his body, from his toes all the way up to his neck.

But what an unbelievable recovery! Denise recalls the doctors' initial diagnosis: "They said he probably would not survive. Then they said that if he did, he would be in a drug-induced coma for several weeks and would probably be in the hospital for up to a year." Unbelievably, Kyle was in intensive care for only two weeks and was released from the hospital only four weeks after his accident.

Steven and Denise say the hospital staff was tremendous. They were all pulling for Kyle, and his recovery amazed the medical professionals.

But Kyle wasn't out of the woods yet. "Twice a day, my parents would have to redo my wrappings," he says. "And that was really painful because all the wounds were open and they would dry into the gauze. Then Mom and Dad would have to rip it out and that was really painful." In addition, his eyes quickly developed cataracts, a sign that his body had been electrocuted. So there were other necessary medical procedures over the following months.

Today, Kyle is in public high school and a member of the National Honor Society. He plays the violin and runs track. Appropriately, his teammates call him "Flash."

His parents are quick to point out God's involvement in their ordeal. The ambulance that took Kyle to the hospital was already in the area because of a false call. They arrived on the scene in less than four minutes.

The baby-sitter who gave Kyle CPR right away had just finished a medical emergency refresher course for an upcoming missions trip at her church. In the end, the trip never happened. Steven and Denise feel God prepared her specifically to be there to help their son.

The doctors said that the immediate help Kyle received was crucial in his recovery. If the ambulance had arrived later, or if CPR had not started minutes after the lightning strike, Kyle would not have made it.

"They told us another minute or two and Kyle would probably never have made it," Steven says. "Another minute or two before they got his breathing and his heart going he would've been dead."

Kyle's body healed at an astonishingly rapid rate. When the plastic wrap was removed from the large skin graft areas, the grafts were 100 percent successful—a rarity for a major skin graft procedure. Other areas that the doctors were considering for additional skin graft work healed on their own.

The Joneses are also amazed at all of the love people gave to them. Local professional sports figures, neighbors, friends from church, and business and school acquaintances all gave unbelievable support to the Jones family. Months of home-cooked meals were brought to the house. Money was donated to help with uncovered medical expenses. Kyle's recovery was a total church and community effort.

The day of the accident, there had been a baby dedication at their church service that morning. On their way home, Kyle and Matthew asked their father if they had been dedicated as children. Steven told them they had both been dedicated to the Lord, not only at church but also in the hospital. "I especially remember Matthew, just a couple of hours old, and we prayed and said, 'Lord, he is Your child.'

"When I saw Kyle on the ground in the woods, it was an instant reminder of what we had talked about in the car. All I said was, 'God, he is Your child and if You take him, that's fine. If it's Your will to heal him, so be it.'"

"I guess I see God's love for me from a whole different perspective," Denise says. "It just means something more to me now to think that He would give up His Son to pay for my sins, because I almost lost my own son. I know how difficult it was to come to the point to be able to say, 'He's not mine, God. He's Yours.' It makes me understand God's sacrifice— and it makes me love Him that much more."

BETH ELLIS

Beth's Real-Life Drama

I heard the newscaster say, "West London police are trying to identify the body of a young man found stabbed to death on the footpath of the Grand Union canal."

In my sixteen years in television, there have been occasions when I've been in the limelight. In college, I studied acting and performed in some rather lavish stage productions. I've performed enough to know that life in the spotlight can be an emotional trap.

The applause is intoxicating. All the attention one gets on the set can be extremely dangerous. Sometimes it is easy to feel you are more important than anyone else because you are the one in front of the audience or camera. Satan's awful sin of pride and self-centeredness can easily begin to take center stage in your heart.

Beth Ellis of London would be the first to admit she was self-centered as an actress. "The most important thing in my life was me. And oh, was I going to make fame and celebrity and all those things that the world so admires today!"

Beth, a gifted actress, trained at the prestigious Royal Academy of the Dramatic Arts. Her acting career began in Northern Ireland, where she worked with the Belfast Arts Theater and then the Ulster Group Theater. She later went into television and hosted her own weekly women's show.

She met a handsome Irish actor named Jimmy, and they married and moved to London. He became a television star for the BBC. She landed a role on a soap opera. They lived life in the fast lane. "Unfortunately, because of success, it was very much a party time. Our friends were people like ourselves: completely self-centered. We really just wanted to make a name for ourselves. We wanted to see our names above the footlights."

With both of their acting careers in high gear, the marriage started to unravel. Step by step the drinking and the life of fame tore her family apart. When they divorced, the couple had two sons, Adam and Hugo, and a beautiful daughter named Amanda. Beth deeply loved her children, but she was determined to keep her career on track. "I went on trying to keep my career going and it did. I loved it. I loved acting. I loved performing. But it was difficult because there were three children as well."

Working with the Royal National Theater, Beth was on tour a good deal of the time. She also landed some impressive roles in West End productions. Her life was constantly on the move, shifting from one theater to the next, one touring company to the next. It gave her little time to lead a normal life. She decided to send her two boys to boarding school so that they could have some continuity in their lives.

Little did she know that when Adam entered the school, he would be required to attend a daily chapel service. Her oldest son, Adam, became a Christian.

Years after he left boarding school, Adam settled in London. One night he never returned home. His roommates were concerned and told his girlfriend. She decided to call Adam's mother.

Beth recalls that fateful phone call with extreme clarity. "His girlfriend had rung me that particular evening. It was in August 1988. And she said, 'Beth, did Adam spend the night with you last night?' And I said, 'No, why?' She said, 'Well, his roommates say he didn't come home, and we are supposed to be going to Albert Hall.'

"And just at that moment, because I had left the television news on, I heard the newscaster say, 'West London police are trying to identify the body of a young man found stabbed to death on the footpath of the Grand Union canal, apparently while fishing.'"

Even though Beth knew of Adam's intense love of fishing, she could not accept the idea that this murder victim might be her son. But she felt compelled to call the police to make sure. "Well, I mean it was a coincidence that one wanted to avoid. I said to his girlfriend, 'I just heard this terrible news. Of course, it isn't Adam. But I've got to ring 9-9-9.' Which is the telephone number for emergency police calls here.

"After examining the photographs of Adam that Beth provided, the police officers said, 'We're sorry, Mrs. Ellis: This is your son. Do you recognize this?' They produced a watch, which I knew immediately. It was my last birthday present to

Adam. So suddenly, instead of being the mother of three, I was the mother of two."

Once the police completed their investigation, they were able to make an intelligent guess as to the details of Adam's murder. His girlfriend had left him by the Grand Canal in London that day while his murderer watched him from a nearby bridge. While Adam stood there holding his rod and reel, waiting for a fish to bite, the horrible drama unfolded.

Once Adam was alone, the criminal placed a brick in a sock and used this crude weapon to knock him off of his feet. Once he had him down, the attacker used Adam's own fishing knife to stab him to death. The motive for the murder was apparently robbery. However, the attacker must have panicked during the murder because he took Adam's wallet but left his valuable watch. Adam only had two English pounds in his pocket. He was murdered for less than five American dollars.

Beth was emotionally crushed. She called Adam's pastor to help her with the funeral arrangements. "He came round and prayed with me. He told me that for many years Adam had prayed for the rest of his family to come to the Lord. That funeral was an extraordinary emotional time for us all. And from that moment onwards Adam's pastor often came round to talk with me about Jesus."

But one day Beth reached her boiling point. She was extremely bitter, and she lashed out at the preacher. "I questioned him quite angrily. I remember saying to him, 'Don't talk to me about a loving God! How could a loving God allow this son of mine, who was a committed Christian, who loved Him, who wanted to be as much like Him as he could—why should He allow him to be struck down?'"

The pastor's answer surprised her. He said, "Beth, the Lord never wanted this. The Lord wanted the world to be this paradise, as in Genesis. But because of our willfulness and because of the way we wanted to have our own way in the world, evil came into the world. Evil was stalking on that canal bank where Adam was that evening. But now, Beth, it is up to you what you're going to do with this." At that, Beth felt the anger and bitterness begin to melt from her heart.

As the pastor was leaving Beth's flat, he encouraged her to pray. He said, "Beth, I'm leaving you now. But I have an enormous feeling that the presence of the Holy Spirit is here. Please, will you kneel down and ask the Lord into your life? Ask the Lord to take care of Adam, because Adam is okay now. Then ask Him to guide your life."

In the quietness of that moment, this heartbroken mother knelt by her couch and prayed. "I believe that's when the Lord came into my life. The Holy Spirit started to take over for me."

Everything became new to her. Her anger, bitterness, and frustrations were lifted. She loved going to church. "I saw these young people worshiping a God that I had never known. And the tears just rolled down my cheeks. I thought, this is where Adam used to come, with all these young people with their arms in the air worshiping a God that they really wanted to praise and thank for their creation. Why didn't I know about this?"

It was during this time that Beth heard about an organization called Youth With A Mission (YWAM). At the age of sixty, Beth decided to go to the mission field.

After a life of self-centeredness and celebrity, Beth was given an unusual assignment. She was put in charge of "hospitality" at an eight-bedroom guest house. Now here this woman was, used to extravagant parties and the high life, now in charge of changing the bedsheets, cleaning the toilets, and vacuuming.

"I remember saying, 'Lord, why at my age do You want me stripping all these beds and doing all this physical, hard work?' And He said, 'It's not your bed-stripping expertise I want, Beth. It's that servant's heart of yours, that looking after other people.'

"In the fifteen months that I was there, so many times I wanted to leave. But I didn't. I really believe the Lord did more in me while stripping beds and looking after others than He could've done in any grand ministry. I'm glad I did it."

Beth traveled all over the world working for YWAM. When she returned home to London, she was offered a major role in the popular West End production *Mousetrap*. "I read for the part and I got it. It was a six-month contract. Suddenly there I was again, in dressing room number one."

But the thrill of performance didn't have the hold on Beth's heart that it once had. There were so many more important commitments in her life now. She loved Bible studies and fellowship and time with family. After the six-month run was completed, the show's management offered to renew Beth's contract. She opted to leave the show.

"I said, 'No. No. These six months have been great, but I want to move on and do something else.' So I didn't stay on. I love the theater and I love theater people. But I also love the people of the world that I'm in. And I had more to talk to them about."

What of her feelings toward the man who murdered her son? "The whole center of our belief and Jesus' commandment to us is to forgive those who have sinned against us. People often say to me, 'How can you forgive somebody who killed your son?' But I don't know. I honestly don't know, except that I think it's Jesus that did it for me."

Beth is now working full time with YWAM in England. She loves the time she spends mentoring Christian young people. Here and there she still gets to perform, and she's recently been involved with some radio dramas for Focus on the Family.

"I've got this wonderful opportunity now to share not Shakespeare's words or Ibsen's words, however wonderful they are, but the words of Christ."

DARWIN BENJAMIN

Darwin the Dart, the Roadrunner Benjamin

Drugs will take you further than you want to go,
cost you more than you're willing to pay, and
keep you longer than you're willing to stay.

Like many teenagers that grow up in the glitz of sunny Southern California, Darwin Benjamin wanted it all. He longed for fame, power, and money. He wanted to be recognized. He wanted to make his parents proud.

His high school nickname was "Darwin the Dart, the Roadrunner Benjamin." He was Inglewood's hometown football hero. The roar of the crowds filled his head like a narcotic.

With football at his side, Darwin was living his dream. "I went to Inglewood High School from 1970 to 1974. I was a high school All-American premier running back. I rushed over a thousand yards three years in a row. It made me feel like I owned Inglewood. I got respect from the teachers. People weren't looking any more at my black skin. It made me feel important. I had the success, the fame, the notoriety, the reputation I always wanted. I was living high on the hog."

After graduating from high school, Darwin looked forward to college, thinking he'd continue being the gridiron hero. But when he attended the University of the Pacific, the cheering crowds from his high school days faded. He hadn't realized he'd be starting over. Darwin found himself sitting on the bench.

"My high school football coach was an image maker. The college football coaches were image breakers. They thought Northern California ball players were better than Southern California ball players. When I got there I had never sat the bench before. But there I found myself, even though I felt I was probably the best or second best player on the team. All I wanted to do was play ball." The lack of recognition started to break his spirit.

When he graduated from college, Darwin's life was rushing toward disaster. Though his parents had taught him strong family values and he longed to make them proud, still he felt the dark pull of partying and, eventually, drugs.

"I was afraid to go back home because everybody expected me to make it to professional football. But I didn't make it. When I left the University of the Pacific in 1978, I began to get involved in drugs.

"Instead of carrying a football, I was carrying drugs. I would be caught on occasion carrying ten grams of cocaine and five grams of crank." *Crank* is the street name for a very harsh form of speed. "My drink was cognac with beer chasers. People would show up at my house for parties. There would be a lot of drugs and the back bedrooms would be open. I was a womanizer or a wannabe lady's pimp. I found myself getting verbally and physically abusive with my women.

"I was trying to live a dream that I hadn't accomplished. I was living for the moment of the drugs to keep my dream of being recognized alive. I wanted the fame, the power, the reputation, and the women.

"The drugs made you feel important. They made you feel valuable. They made you feel that you were priceless, that the party couldn't take place without you and that they needed to have you around."

Darwin's life was on a downward spiral. His wild life of drugs and partying intensified to a dangerous level. But one day he met a beautiful Hispanic woman named Yolanda—and she captured his heart.

"I saw her and I got interested. She was my big ten, my Bo Derek. She looked good. She had nice hair and gold earrings on. I was just captivated and challenged. I knew this was somebody I wanted to be with."

Yolanda and Darwin seemed to be a perfect match: They both loved to party. But their wild lifestyle brought with it distrust and infidelity. Their relationship was filled with intense jealousy and violence.

"The only thing that we really had in common in our relationship was drugs and sex. I found myself saying that I loved her, but there was physical and verbal abuse. Our relationship was so violent, one day I chased her through a window and she tried running me down with a car. She would catch me in a hotel room being intimate with different women. Like I said, sex was about the only thing we had in common."

Their relationship took a strange turn when Yolanda got

pregnant. Darwin was extremely unsupportive. He even refused to go with her to the hospital for the delivery.

"She had told me that she was pregnant, but I was so strung out on the drugs I didn't want to accept that fact. I was sitting up after a party at my house and she called and asked me to be with her as she brought our kid into the world. I told her no. I hung up the phone and I started to take more coke and crank.

"And I was just doing the alcohol, the drugs, and the partying. Then you find out that the drugs will take you further than you want to go, cost you more than you're willing to pay, and keep you longer than you're willing to stay."

Darwin's mother-in-law demanded that he take her to the hospital so she could be at her daughter's side. When they arrived at the hospital, Darwin felt something very strange. They had missed the delivery, and out in the parking lot he saw an emergency incubator being rolled into the hospital. Something told him to follow that incubator.

"So I followed the incubator through the parking lot, through the double doors down to the elevator. We got to the sixth floor and I was greeted by a doctor. He said, 'You must be Darwin Benjamin.' He took me to the maternity ward. I went in and I saw a beautiful half black and half Hispanic child. She had my eyes. There was no denying that she was mine. I was amazed at the resemblance and I was excited."

When Darwin saw his daughter for the first time, his heart filled with joy and pride. It was one of the most moving experiences in his life. But his joy soon turned to sorrow. His beautiful baby girl was a twin, and her twin sister was not so lucky. The emergency incubator Darwin had seen in the parking lot was for her. She suffered from severe deformities.

When he rounded the corner and saw his second daughter, his heart stopped and tears filled his eyes. Several of her organs had formed on the outside of her body. Her eyes were swollen shut. Her head was twice the size of a normal baby's. Her left side was paralyzed and her chest was crushed. There was a cyst that ran from the lower part of her head down to the lower part of her back.

And then came the moment that will haunt Darwin's mind forever. "I remember putting my right index finger into where she was lying, and she grabbed it with her right hand even though her eyes were swollen shut. It was like she was saying to me, 'Daddy, oh, Daddy, help me. Oh, how it hurts. I know it's you, Daddy.' And I pulled my hand away from her hand and I touched my coat. I felt the coke and the crank in my pocket, the stuff that I had been doing, and I knew instantly that they had contributed to my daughter's deformity."

The medical teams battled to save his daughter's life. For five days this little girl fought bravely to stay alive. But the end finally came. When it did, Darwin ran to his daughter's side.

"I pulled the IV off of her arms and her head. I wrapped the blanket around her and I held her in my arms. I said, 'Baby, I'm so sorry. I'm so sorry, baby, for what I've done to you. Your daddy is going to get his life together and be with you in the kingdom of God.'

"I don't know why I said that because I wasn't even serving the Lord. But for the first time in her five-day life it was like a peace came upon her. She struggled with all of her energy and opened her eyes. She looked at me, I looked at her, and then she smiled. She took one last breath, gave a deep sigh, and died in my arms."

When she died, a part of Darwin's heart died, too. He became cold and angry. He blamed Yolanda for their daughter's death.

But God began to work in their lives. Family members were tirelessly praying for Darwin and Yolanda. God began to knock on the door of Darwin's heart. He used an old college partying buddy named Donny Moore. Donny had become a preacher. Darwin had to see how this friend's life could change so drastically.

So Darwin went to hear Donny preach. At the end of the service he went forward to pray. "All I know is that I felt warmth and I felt the love of God. And I know that on that day—November 13, 1988, at 7:45 P.M.—the Lord saved me, healed me, filled me, and delivered me. I've been clean now for thirteen years.

"I renewed my vows with my wife to do it right. And He saved my wife. He restored my family. He put me in ministry. Even though it's been thirteen years, it still seems like yesterday."

Yolanda thanks God every day for her new husband. "I know his stand for Jesus is uncompromising. His first love is the Lord. I really admire that because I know he's going to cover us and protect us. I know that he's there for us. He's firm in his belief. His standards are high for his family, which brings the challenge to all of us to set the standard up higher. I'm grateful for that because there's a constant challenge in our walk."

Darwin and Yolanda now reach out to those who are caught in the darkness of drugs. Darwin has worked extensively with a unique evangelistic team called Radical Reality.

He's also done extensive work in reaching out to troubled youth. And together Darwin and Yolanda run Truth Ministries, which reaches out to families that are broken by the pain of abortion.

"I thank God for His love because without His love I wouldn't even stand a chance," Darwin says. "I thank Him for His mercy. I thank Him for my family. I thank Him for the simple things such as food, clothing, and shelter. I thank Him for His Son and the Cross. I thank Him for the shedding of blood and that I have a direct line to the Father through the Son. I'm thankful that He's willing to listen to me and He's willing to talk to me. The communication is probably what I'm thankful for most of all—that He'll meet all my needs."

MARILYN BURLEIGH

The Night Our House Blew Away

As the tornado came closer to us, we could hear the trees popping.
It sounded more like a freight train, but
louder than a freight train.
It sounded like a 747 going over our heads.

Several years ago I saw three waterspouts over the Chesapeake Bay. They were all in a row, moving hauntingly, slowly across the horizon. A friend said it looked like the fingers of God.

A twister is one of the most awe-inspiring forces of nature. Tornadoes can drive a piece of straw deep into a solid piece of wood, snap a giant oak tree like a matchstick, and rip a slab of pavement off of the roadway in front of you.

You are about to meet a family that came face-to-face with the full force and fury of a massive twister. It forever changed their lives.

It was November 21, 1992, the Saturday before Thanksgiving. Marilyn Burleigh was in her Wilson, Louisiana, home on that muggy night with her two children, Lynée, age eleven, and Brian, age seven. Her husband, Randy, was at work.

She had been listening to an out-of-state football game on the radio. Lynée had watched a movie on video and Brian was sick in bed, complaining of a stomachache. None of them had heard the local weather warnings.

It was about nine-thirty. Their lights had gone out, so Marilyn was using a flashlight to feed her dog, Shelby.

"I walked to the back door and put the dog's food down. It was still very muggy feeling and warm but I didn't notice anything unusual. I walked back down the hall to the bedroom. And I'd just gotten back to the bedroom when I heard an unusual sound in the distance. It sounded like a little roar. And I stopped and thought, what is that? Then I heard it again and instantly, I guess by instinct, I knew it was a tornado."

The Burleighs had practiced tornado drills with their children, so Lynée and Brian knew what to do. Marilyn called her kids into the hallway and hurried them into an interior closet.

"When I got the closet door open the pressure was already so low and the roar was getting louder. The pressure was so low that it was trying to suck out a box in the top of the closet. The kids got in the closet. I got in on top of them. And before I could get the door shut, the roof popped."

The roof was literally ripped off the walls of their home. Marilyn and her children were now inside one of the largest tornadoes ever to hit that part of Louisiana. The local weather bureau was clocking this twister's winds at over two hundred miles per hour.

Marilyn was afraid that the walls of the closet might collapse in on them, so she wedged herself inside as tightly as possible. She placed her shoulder firmly against one wall and then braced her feet against the other side of the closet. She hung on to her children with both arms.

Marilyn will never forget the haunting sounds of the twister as it closed in on her defenseless family: "At first from a distance it sounded like a roar, then like barrels rolling. As the tornado came closer to us we could hear the trees popping. It sounded more like a freight train, but louder than a freight train. It sounded like a 747 going over our heads.

"But the worst sound I heard was after the roof came off the house. As the wind came through, you could hear the two-by-fours and the rafters break and crash as they fell down. And it seemed like it was the loudest sound because this was our home being totally destroyed. It seemed to echo. The pressure was so low, it seemed like our eardrums were being sucked out."

The seconds passed in slow motion. It seemed the tornado roared and pulled at them forever. "You just kind of hang on and say, 'Oh, Jesus, oh, Jesus, oh, Jesus.' You just call His name. You don't have time to think."

Their nightmarish ordeal ended just as abruptly as it had begun. There was a lull in the storm's intensity, and Marilyn thought for a moment that it was over. But she soon realized they were inside the "eye" of the tornado. Just like hurricanes, twisters have a calm center core. When the back side of the tornado hit, the walls of the closet began to move.

Marilyn, Lynée, and Brian literally were lifted off the ground for a short time. Marilyn recounts, "The whole thing probably took a minute at the most, but it seemed like it took forever because it was in slow motion. We went forward about six to eight feet. Then we sort of went sideways four or five feet. And we went backwards about eight or ten feet. We probably traveled maybe twenty-five feet. We ended up in the other room.

"The kids were literally ripped out of my arms by the twister. When the closet started moving my first thought was, my babies are going to die and there is nothing I can do about it. I felt so totally helpless. But then I realized God was in control, and it was at that moment He told me, 'I'm still here. I hear you. I am with you.'

"I felt like there was somebody else in that closet. It was a physical presence, like an angel almost. The kids have said the same thing. We felt like we had arms around us protecting us. We could feel the arms. Both children have said that they felt arms that they knew were not mine. From then on, even though we were flying through the air, I had no fear. We just knew that God was there. He was in control and it was going to be okay."

The twister finally roared away on its destructive path. The winds died down and Marilyn felt rain falling gently on her face. The closet was gone. The roof was gone. Their home was destroyed. Marilyn called for Lynée and Brian. From the darkness nearby she heard their voices, calmly calling back to her.

Miraculously, Marilyn, Lynée, and Brian had made it through the tornado without a scratch. Even Shelby the dog had made it through the ordeal unhurt. She evidently had wedged herself low to the ground between the patio and the back wall of the house.

Marilyn was soon able to get word to Randy that they were okay.

He remembers the eerie journey home that night in the moonlight. "I got half a mile from the house and the trees and power lines were down, so I had to stop the vehicle and start walking. It was drizzling at the time. When I got to the house—I should say the lot, more or less—the moon was coming up. I could see that all that was standing was the north wall of the house."

After a tearful reunion, Randy and Marilyn stood in shock before the rubble that had once been their home. Later, daylight revealed the scope of the devastation. Almost all of their earthly belongings were gone, destroyed.

"It looked like a war zone," Marilyn says. "It was so unbelievable. When you see it at night it looks bad enough. But the next day everything is in the ditches as far as you can see, and what trees are left have things in them. Our wheelbarrow was hanging from a transformer pole. The bushes down along the fencerow were coated with pink insulation. It was unbelievable. You knew it was bad but you didn't realize it was that bad."

Inside the north wall of the house, the only wall left standing, was a small two-by-two-foot closet. The ceiling was intact. Inside were the Burleigh family's picture albums. A lifetime of family memories was protected from the tornado by this little closet. Marilyn felt God spared their precious family mementos. "That was the only place in the entire house that didn't get wet. And that is where we had all the baby pictures, the pictures you can't replace."

The Burleighs found bits and pieces of their lives scattered all over the region. Brian had a sandbox with some small

Fisher-Price toys in it. Their boy's little treasures ended up in someone's pasture about fifteen miles away, all in a row.

The furious winds had bent a basketball pole in their yard down to the ground. The metal pole was filled with concrete and anchored in a concrete footing that went six feet underground. They couldn't bend the post back up. They finally had to literally dig the basketball goal up, footing and all, to move it.

The Burleighs' car was moved out from under the carport and across the yard. "A small tree had blown down and the car was propped up on the sycamore tree," Marilyn remembers. "All the windows were blown out. The car was full of pond water and pine straw."

After the tornado, the family lived in temporary housing miles from their property in Wilson. "One day a man drove up and said, 'I've got a Louisiana license plate with current tags,'" Randy says. "He said I might be able to return it to the owner because the tags were valid. I looked at the back and saw a piece of familiar looking duct tape. When Marilyn showed up, I said, 'You'd better sit down because you aren't going to believe this!'"

That piece of duct tape held the spare key to their pond-water flooded car. It was their own license plate. The plate had been ripped off the car but had not bent and the bolts on the car had not been damaged. The license plate had literally been shaken off by the force of the wind and then thrown fifteen miles, where the man found it.

Marilyn and Randy both feel that God taught them valuable lessons through their tragedy. "Count your blessings," Randy says. "Be grateful for what you've got. One minute they can be here and the next minute they can be gone. Don't hold on to your valuables."

Marilyn adds: "The things God made that can never be replaced because they're unique creations, He spared. You can't replace your children. You can't replace your family pet. They're special. Anything else you can replace. You can go to Wal-Mart and buy a new one."

When the Burleighs rebuilt their home on their property, they made one modification. "If Randy had been home, there wouldn't have been enough room for him," Marilyn says, laughing. So this time they made the new reinforced closet a "four-seater."

Turning thoughtful, Marilyn says, "I learned that there is nothing so big that God can't handle it. No matter where you are He knows where you are—and He can find you and protect you."

ERIC AND DANNELL ANSCHUETZ

The Power of a Praying Army

Eric went into cardiac arrest. His lungs totally failed.
His kidneys had failed. His liver had failed.
The skin was failing because it was peeling off.
His heart stopped.

In March of 1993, Eric Anschuetz was stationed at the Naval Air Station in Dallas, Texas. To stay in shape, he rode his bike back and forth to work. One particular afternoon the sky was gray and overcast. As he was cutting across the end of a runway on the way home, an F-14 fighter jet seemed to pop right out of a low cloud bank.

"It was making a lot of noise. It startled me. I was watching that jet come down right in front of me instead of watching where I was going. I rode off the edge of the road and fell. I flipped over the handlebars and cut my knee. I just got scuffed up a bit, nothing major." He went home, showered, and treated his minor cuts and scratches.

"I guess it was about a week later that I got sick. I thought I had the flu. I was nauseated and had a high fever."

As his sickness progressed, some unusual symptoms developed. "I felt like I had a sunburn on my back and the top of my head. Then the skin on my hands was peeling off. It was just turning white and peeling off. I had diarrhea. I was vomiting."

After forty-eight hours, Eric went to the naval clinic. His blood pressure was extremely low. They treated him for his flu symptoms and released him once his blood pressure stabilized. They encouraged him to come back if he didn't feel better in the morning.

The next day Eric's symptoms worsened. His wife, Dannell, felt it was time to take him to the hospital. "Saturday morning when we got up he was still very ill," she says. "He couldn't hold anything down. He was having fevers and chills. He just wasn't himself. I insisted that he go to the emergency room. As we were on our way, he was talking kind of crazy. It just was like a severe case of the flu and being very dehydrated."

His illness was also starting to affect his vision. Little did she know that her husband's body was literally starting to shut down. The ER personnel ran some tests and felt Eric's condition was getting serious. They sent him to an infectious disease specialist. Dannell braced for the worst.

"Afterwards the doctor came out and told me that she felt he had toxic shock syndrome. He had liver failure, kidney failure, renal failure, and then his skin was also involved. He went into the intensive care unit on Saturday and really got progressively worse."

Toxic shock syndrome is usually thought of as a woman's

disease. It begins with an infection that eventually starts shutting down a person's body organ by organ. That is why Eric's skin was falling off and his sight was starting to fail. They concluded he must've gotten the infection when he took his spill on his bicycle.

By the following Tuesday, Eric's chances of recovery seemed bleak. Dannell contacted a doctor friend, who immediately researched Eric's situation and came to examine Eric. This physician and her fiancé, a cardiologist, went in to see Eric.

When they came out to Dannell in the waiting room, the news was not good. "Linda looked at me and said, 'He's really sick, Dannell.' And I said, 'I know he's really sick. Linda, they won't tell me anything.'

"Linda looked at her fiancé, and he shook his head. She turned back to me and said, 'Dannell, I think that if he doesn't make a turnaround in the next two hours he's not going to make it.'

"And two hours after she left, almost to the minute, Eric went into cardiac arrest. His lungs totally failed. His kidneys had failed. His liver had failed. The skin was failing because it was peeling off. His heart stopped."

Dannell knew that, short of a miracle, Eric was going to die. So she set a powerful spiritual force into motion. There was a massive network of friends and relatives all over the country praying for Eric. Dannell also notified the Order of Saint Luke, where a special prayer session was held for Eric throughout the night.

"There was this man at our church who didn't know about Eric's condition that night," Dannell remembers. "But he felt God calling him to go to the chapel to pray for Eric. When he got to the church, he found out about Eric's crisis."

There was a group at the hospital praying. Others were praying in a chapel. There truly was an army of people praying for Eric throughout that night.

As the prayers intensified, so did Eric's condition. After he was revived from an initial heart failure that night, Eric's heart went into cardiac arrest for a second time. Everything looked hopeless. Dannell had nothing she could hold onto except her faith. Through her tears, she begged God to heal her husband. People all over the country were praying that same prayer.

Late that night, Dannell began to see God's miracle. About three hours after going into cardiac arrest, Eric woke up with Dannell at his side.

"I remember waking up at midnight," Eric says. "I remember Dannell was there hugging me and saying, 'Everything's gonna be all right now. Everything's gonna be all right.' And I'm thinking, What are you talking about? There's this guy from our church kneeling on the bed next to me and I'm thinking, What are you doing? All of a sudden he says, 'It's a miracle!' And I'm thinking, What's a miracle? I had no idea what was going on."

Eric had made it through the most dangerous time and was beginning the slow journey toward health. After that night, Eric passed out again for five more days. But even then it was clear he was going to be all right.

As the weeks went by everyone began to be amazed at his recovery. Doctors believed Eric would need to be on dialysis for months, maybe even as long as half a year. But Eric was taken off dialysis after only twenty-four days. He was told he wouldn't be able to go to work for six to eight weeks, but Eric went back to work for half-days after only a month.

Dannell—now a doctor herself—is still overwhelmed at her husband's total healing. "They told us his kidneys would never be completely normal again. They went back to normal. His liver went back to normal. His lungs went back to normal. There's absolutely nothing on the X rays now. His heart went back to normal. Just recently Eric had a cardiac stress testing—100 percent normal. That just doesn't happen, you know?"

Dannell feels she learned some amazing spiritual lessons from her husband's illness. "I think the most important lesson that I learned was that I had to let God take control of the situation and that God is in control. I'm a controlling person. I'm a physician now because I wanted to control the situation. I wanted what I wanted. I wanted the outcome to be what I wanted it to be.

"What God taught me through many spiritual people at that time was that I had to release Eric into His hands and that His will was to be done. And I had to accept it no matter what it was. Learning to depend and trust in the Lord no matter what the outcome—that was a big thing for me."

Eric says, "God has made me realize just how personal He is. No matter where we find ourselves, He is there and He is in total control."

DAVID HOLDEN

The Calling of David:
Step by Step

*There was a burning in my hands, running up to my elbows....
It wasn't just the heating of the room or palpitations in my body.
It was something quite supernatural.*

D o you think that in a single instant God could totally redirect your life?

For years we've all heard miraculous stories of how God has called people to do some amazing things. There was the famous southern preacher who, while eating a chicken salad sandwich with his wife, got the call of God to build a Bible college. Pat Robertson wrote a book on how God called him to build a world-reaching television ministry—and at the time he had only seventy dollars and didn't even own a television set!

But I don't personally know anyone who has had a more dramatic or inspiring calling on his life than David Holden. His story is truly amazing.

David, a humble and thoughtful man, lives in East Sussex, England. After becoming a Christian later in life, he left a successful seventeen-year career in real estate to follow the Lord's call to Bible college. He overcame many trials and hurdles to achieve his ultimate goal of becoming a pastor.

Upon graduation, he set out on a mission to touch as many lives as possible. After eighteen months of tireless—but volunteer—service to a certain congregation, David requested to become a paid staff member. The request was rejected.

David was devastated. How could things turn out the way they did? His wife, Sheila, had sacrificed and supported him through his long years of Bible study. David had even sold his real estate business in order to follow God's will. Now what were they going to do?

One lonely night, David decided to go to a special church meeting. Little did he know this meeting would totally change the rest of his life. At the close of the service the pastor insisted that someone needed to come forward.

David's head was bowed in prayer but when he looked up his incredible experience began. "I found as I opened my eyes that the pastor was pointing at me and he said, 'It's you and your name is David. God is about to anoint you for the work He's called you to do.' At this point he said, 'Stand up.' As I stood I felt an incredible sort of rush of the Spirit into me. I can't explain it, but very shortly afterward I found myself on the floor with a tremendous power running through my hands. I couldn't move. I was literally pinned to the ground."

For forty minutes, David says God was speaking to him, impressing on him what He wanted him to do. "And from that point on I can't tell you a lot of what was going on around me because it was as though I were locked in with God. He began to speak to me. It was quite terrifying in one way and yet incredibly awesome in another. As I lay on the floor, God said He had called me to paint.

"It began to dawn on me that He was talking about art. Now, that thrilled me, but at the same time it rather concerned me because I'd never really painted anything in my life before. And I'd certainly had no interest in art up to that point."

But David remembers a strange sensation in his body. "There was a burning in my hands, running up to my elbows. It was almost painful, it was so strong. It felt as though I had been plugged into an electrical supply. It wasn't just the heating of the room or palpitations in my body. It was something quite supernatural."

When his encounter ended, David picked himself up off of the floor and returned home to Sheila. Imagine her surprise when her middle-aged husband came home and announced that he was now an artist. She knew David better than anyone else. She knew that he didn't have one artistic bone in his body.

"Well, I have to say I was somewhat skeptical," Sheila says. "From where I was sitting it was a bit of a harebrained scheme. I'm afraid I was not exactly overly enthusiastic when he announced it." To start a new career at his age without any previous art training seemed insane.

David agreed with his wife. He felt that God must've called the wrong person. Up to that point he had never dreamed of being an artist. "I didn't have any kind of inclination or desire to paint—that's the strange thing. Often as children you doodle or you scratch around with a pencil or crayon and brushes. I never did this. Why that was the case I don't know, but it may be because I was never really encouraged in that. Neither of my parents was artistic in that way. I just didn't naturally gravitate toward it. I didn't even have an interest in art."

But David realized that if this calling was truly from God then the proof would be in the artwork. So obediently, he took his first step. David went out and bought paper and some paints. Then he just sat down and started painting. "It felt like it was somebody else painting through me. It didn't feel as though it was me. It wasn't a learned process. It came so easily and it wasn't a struggle. It was just something that came out of me and I wanted to do it."

When Sheila saw her husband paint these watercolor landscapes, she was shocked. "I was amazed at the quality of the paintings that he began to produce immediately. I was absolutely astonished."

David was just as surprised as his wife. Within a three-month period he produced thirty-eight paintings. He and Sheila decided that he should put on an art show. They wanted to see what the public thought of his newfound talent, so they rented a local exhibition hall and Sheila asked God for some specific results.

"I just said to the Lord, 'Look, if this is really of You, I'm just going to ask that David will get back all of the money that he has spent to date. That is my fleece to You, Lord. If this is right, You've got to at least get us back to the break-even point. Then, if we're back to even, we can trust You for the next step.'"

At the exhibition, some viewers were moved to tears while looking at David's work. His watercolor landscapes of the

English countryside were a strong success.

"He actually sold about two-thirds of his paintings," Sheila says. "I thought that was amazing. Afterwards, when we added up what he'd sold and subtracted what he'd spent in getting to that point, we found we had actually broken even. In fact, we had made a very, very small profit. That was the real turning point for me."

It has now been six years since that initial exhibition. When art collectors ask him how long he's been painting, they always seem surprised by his answer.

"I'm tempted to say, 'You're not going to believe me.' They often ask where I've been for training. 'Which art school or art college did you go to? Royal Academy?' I try to explain I haven't had any formal training. But then I bring in this dimension that God has gifted me to do that. It happened quite suddenly in a short period of time and quite unexpectedly to me. They are amazed because a lot of people think I've been painting all my life. When they see the work they think that's all I've ever done."

David loves God's new calling in his life. "When I paint I feel the pleasure of God. And there are many parts of Scripture that come to me when I meditate on that. The pleasure God has in looking down on what He has made. He takes pleasure in us. And He rejoices over us. It gives Him such pleasure to see one of His creation just lost in the gifting He's given. It brings glory to Him as that gift is used. And so I love painting for that reason. I feel the intense pleasure of God. I know He has called me to do it."

Both David and Sheila Holden say God has taught them some valuable spiritual lessons. "Just because God has called you to something doesn't mean it's going to be easy," Sheila says. "God called Gideon to fight the Midianites, Joshua to lead the people of Israel, and Daniel to be a leader in a pagan society. Those were all very real callings, but it didn't make it a pushover, you know? Through this whole experience there has just been this sense that we did really know we had that kind of a calling—and we had to hold on and trust that God was leading us."

It's been years since David experienced that dramatic call to be an artist. Hundreds of paintings later, David feels the entire wonderful experience has been totally orchestrated by God every step of the way. "And that is the whole key to my testimony: that God reveals His purposes step by step. It's not all in a sudden rush. He doesn't give you the whole picture to begin with. But gradually He shows you the next step that He wants you to take."

If you'd like to see some of David's paintings, you can go to his Web site: www.cuckfieldgallery.com. My absolute favorite painting is called "Morning Shadows." Other favorites include "Pooh Bridge" and "Rising Water." His inspired English landscapes are both soothing and refreshing.

"When God truly touches a human life," David says, "that person will never ever be the same again. That is what's so incredible about the living God: that He wants to do that. I mean, why should God do that? He could just destroy us. We're people who've lived so much of our lives in our own way. We've fallen short of His standards. He has every right to destroy us. And then He reaches down and does something like this.

"I don't deserve it. You don't deserve it. None of us deserves

His grace—free unmerited favor. It is so incredible what God has for each one of us."

JOHN AND GLENYS SINGER

~♫⊙

The Unbelievable Samaritans

*Her wounds were bleeding uncontrollably and
her body was doubled over in horrible pain.
Her husband had shot her three more times.*

J
ohn and Glenys Singer of Peekskill, New York, lived with
their five daughters in an elegant Victorian home at 45
Welcher Avenue. Their street looked like any normal
American neighborhood. The lawns along the roadway were
dotted with beautifully landscaped greenery and children's
bicycles.

The air was crisp and quiet on this cold January morning
in 1999. John and Glenys's three oldest daughters had gone off
to school that Monday. It was their first day back after the
Christmas holidays. Glenys was upstairs ironing. John began
his day down in the basement reading his Bible.

"I had just settled down to reading the Word," John says,

"and there was this loud bang. It didn't sound normal so I ran upstairs to see what my wife was doing. She looked at me with the same puzzled look. I thought, What happened up here? And she was thinking, Did something blow up in the basement?"

Within seconds the confused couple was swept up into an unbelievable nightmare. John recalls everything happening so incredibly fast. "Just in that moment the front door opened and our neighbor came in. She collapsed right at our feet and said, 'Please help me! He's gonna kill me!'"

Their neighbor, Colleen, was bleeding from a gunshot wound. Her husband was trying to kill her. Glenys sprang into action. She helped Colleen get to her feet and then moved her into a back bedroom. John ran to the phone near their front doorway to call the police. But before he could complete the call, their intense drama took a strange twist.

"I was standing just a few feet from the front door, which was glass, when it just exploded. It sounded like someone used a cannon to just blow the front door to bits. Now all of a sudden whatever was happening was very close."

John's immediate reaction was to get out of the line of fire. He flew down the stairway to the basement, where he called 9-1-1. The next moments were unbearable, and to John they seemed like hours. Through an in-house intercom he talked briefly to Glenys. She told him everything was all right upstairs. John felt utter helplessness when he heard more shots going off.

"I was right near the back door there, so I figured I could go get the police. As soon as I ran out I saw Glenys at the window. I was so relieved to see her there. She was just kind of stunned. I remember saying, 'Jump, jump!' I was in a panic. I saw her hesitate, not knowing at that point she was thinking about the children. And I was just saying, 'You're alive. Jump out!' So she jumped out."

Unbeknownst to John, Glenys had taken Colleen into the same room where their young children were playing. Glenys had wisely hid them in a closet, but as the drama unfolded, Colleen had fallen in front of that closet, preventing Glenys from getting to the girls.

By this time, policemen were taking up positions in the front yard. It was still bitterly cold outside. "I ran over to tell them, I want to go get my kids now. The police grabbed me and said, 'Get down!' I said, 'Come on. Let's go get my kids now. We've got guns. Let's go in there and get this guy. Let's go get my kids!'" The police, wanting to effectively evaluate the situation, refused his request.

Within minutes they saw a feeble figure on the front porch. Somehow Colleen had made it to the front doorway. Her wounds were bleeding uncontrollably and her body was doubled over in horrible pain. Her husband had shot her three more times. Her escape was unbelievable. She made it to the front driveway, where she collapsed. Paramedics rushed her to the hospital.

"Now there was a standoff," John says. "There were helicopters and their SWAT team. I mean, they had everything out there. The house was surrounded, and the street was blocked off. I was pretty panicked. I realized all of a sudden that I was in a helpless, powerless position. Then it just struck me that I needed the Lord and I needed to pray right then!"

Moments after his prayer, John heard something over the

police radio. "I heard someone on the radio say there's two children on the porch. Another officer and I ran up and grabbed my two kids. It was an unbelievable feeling to have those girls back in my arms."

John took his wife and youngest daughters next door to get out of the cold. But then their story took another dark turn. "I remember the look on my neighbor's face. He said, 'John I don't know if I should tell you this, but your house is on fire.'"

The gunman had set fire to the house. At first the police thought he had done this as a diversion so he could escape out the back of the house and into the woods. But he never tried to come out. He had committed suicide and died in the flames.

John stepped outside to watch their house burn. It went quickly. "I saw my house. It was just a big orange ball of flames. The fire department asked me if I had an accelerant in there. One fireman said that in thirty years he'd never seen a house go up that fast."

In a matter of minutes, a lifetime of memories was gone. Irreplaceable family pictures, books, mementos, and most of their belongings were destroyed. The children's toys, all of their clothes, all of their furniture, appliances—gone.

If the Singers' story had ended right there, it would be powerful enough. But what the Singers did next was so unexpected, so out of place in a world in which people look out only for themselves, it drew the attention of the Associated Press.

John and Glenys Singer decided to help with the gunman's funeral. When they found out Colleen's family was having trouble securing a place for her husband's funeral, the Singers volunteered their own church for the funeral services.

And if that were not enough, when the gunman's family

had problems getting someone to preach the funeral, John decided to speak at the ceremony.

The media and the public could not believe what the Singers had done. John and Glenys's Christian love for this man and his family touched the community so deeply that the Singers were literally flooded with donations. People began leaving money and checks on the door of their temporary residence, their church's parsonage. Local stores donated household appliances and toys for the children. Several volunteers from the Singers' church sifted through truckloads of donated clothing. Even their insurance company made sure the Singers were well compensated for their loss.

People from the community weren't the only ones replacing what the Singers had lost. God was involved, too. The one item that John most regretted losing was his Bible. "I had a King James, black leather, Thompson Chain Reference Bible that was given to me when I was an assistant pastor in the church back in the seventies. It was dear to me. When I opened the door to the house that they had put us in and took one step in, I looked on the table right next to the door and there was an exact copy of the Bible that I lost. The exact copy! Nobody knew which Bible I had. But God did. It was just that little sign that said, 'It's Me, son. I'm here. Here's your Bible back.'"

John and Glenys believe God miraculously protected their daughters on that fateful day in January. After their ordeal, Sarah, one of the daughters that was at home that morning, had something she wanted to say to Glenys.

"As I was sitting on the couch at our neighbors', my little daughter came over and tapped me quietly, 'Mom, I was not afraid of the man at all. He just told me, "You can leave now. Don't be afraid of me. Your mom and dad are outside. You may go."' I can't tell you what it was like as a mother to hear those words and know that he didn't traumatize them in any way."

John remembers when the detectives questioned little Sarah. "They asked Sarah if she saw the gunman's face. She said, 'Yes, I saw his face.' Then she volunteered, 'But I didn't look at the gun because I didn't want to.' And that was the first time that I realized that God had shielded them from seeing anything that would scar their memories." To this day, John and Glenys feel they've never seen any negative side effects on either of their two youngest daughters.

Many times, John has wondered whether he made all the right choices that morning. If he'd only made the 9-1-1 call a little faster, maybe he would have been able to stay by Glenys's side. Maybe he could have wrestled the gunman down and gotten the weapon away from him. But in retrospect, John feels each action happened so quickly that God guided him step by step. And he'll always remember what one of the police officers said to him. "The policeman who was crouched down by the van said, 'Hey man, whatever you did, you did it right, because you're all alive.'"

Even after all they lost that day, John and Glenys have a deep hope that the gunman may have had a change of heart and accepted the Lord before he died. Glenys recalls, "I had Scripture on the refrigerator, over the sink, wherever. And my husband and I had our Bibles open in the home. We had inspirational pictures on the walls. Perhaps the gunman saw something, some verse, something from the Word that maybe caught his attention and caused him to just think about Christ, focus his attention on the Lord."

After John spoke at the funeral, the gunman's mother approached him. "She came to me in the aisle there and said, 'I'm ready, Mr. Singer. I'm ready to accept the Lord into my heart.' And she added, 'My husband said to me, "If that Mr. Singer could forgive all this, then I'm coming to church, too."'"

It has been two years since that fateful day in January. The Singers have relocated to New Jersey. Both John and Glenys feel God has totally restored all that the fire took and then some. "I just thank God because of His divine protection," John says. "I believe that God is a very present help in a time of trouble."

When asked what she learned from the ordeal, Glenys replies, "I learned how sovereign God is, how detailed. Oh, just how wonderful it is to watch the hand of God. This was tragic, yet to watch God's hand in it all was just really an awesome thing."

JERRY WOODFILL

The Amazing Journey of Apollo 13

I heard the words from deep space,
"Houston, we had a problem."

There are rare moments in history that seem to stop time. It's as if the whole world seems to hold its breath, waiting to see what is going to happen. I was twelve years old when the dramatic Apollo 13 mission to the moon caught the world's attention. I remember being glued to the television, wondering if the crew was going to make it back to earth or if they were going to be lost to the eternal black void of outer space.

It was April 13, 1970, and Jerry Woodfill was right in the thick of it. He was the Warning System Engineer for the ill-fated Apollo 13 lunar mission that Monday night. Jerry was due to go off his shift at 10 P.M. Just after nine o'clock, he remembers looking down at the control console and realizing that something was terribly wrong.

At that same instant, two hundred thousand miles from Earth, the Apollo 13 astronauts heard a muffled pop. They looked out the port window and saw a vapor venting into outer space.

"That's when I heard the words from deep space, 'Houston, we had a problem.' Of course, in the famous Ron Howard movie the line goes, 'Houston, we *have* a problem.' I guess that indicates a little more immediacy as far as their peril. But they did say, 'Houston, we *had* a problem.' What they should have said, though, was 'Houston, we have *problems*'—because I saw multiple alarm indications come on."

It took the NASA engineers a good while to figure out what had gone wrong. In each Apollo lunar mission there were literally two spacecrafts along for the ride: a command ship, used to orbit the lunar surface and bring the crew back to earth, and a lunar lander, which transported two of the three astronauts to the moon's surface and then returned the men to the orbiting command ship. Apparently, a short circuit had caused an explosion in one of the oxygen tanks on the command vessel. It was the liquid oxygen from the damaged tank that they'd seen venting into space.

"When that oxygen tank blew up, it caused a number of subsequent failures in other systems," Jerry says. "The fuel cells stopped functioning, which took out the electrical power in the command ship. Without electrical power in the command vessel, they had to switch over from the fuel cell power to battery power. The ship was actually dying."

It soon dawned on the NASA personnel what that explosion meant. "I think it took perhaps ninety minutes before we fully understood that the control ship could no longer support life and that we had to use that little lunar landing craft as a lifeboat. The control ship was designed to hold three astronauts and to support them for the whole journey. The lander was designed for only two men and could support them for a mission not longer than forty-eight hours. Now it would have to last the entire time it would take to get back to Earth—with *three* men inside."

With the three astronauts' lives at stake—engineering crews and flight controllers scrambled to find a way to get these brave men home. They faced three major dilemmas. First, the air filtration system in the lunar lander would not be able to sustain three men for the length of time needed to get them home. The crewmen would eventually die from a buildup of carbon dioxide in the ship. Second, without electrical power in the command ship, they would be unable to reenter the Earth's atmosphere.

Third, with the command ship damaged, they could not use the vessel's propulsion engine to take the crew back home. Instead, they would have to use the much smaller engine on the lunar lander. But that engine had been designed only to get that small ship from the command vessel to the surface of the moon and then back to the mother ship. It was never intended to push both spacecrafts over a long journey around the moon and then back to the Earth. They would need to totally rethink the flight plans. Their task seemed overwhelming. Many felt the Apollo 13 astronauts would not be returning home.

But there is an interesting twist to this story. Jerry says that people all around the United States and all over the globe began praying for the safe return of the Apollo 13 crew.

"The prayer was just very evident. They prayed at the

Wailing Wall in Jerusalem. The Pope in Saint Peter's Basilica prayed that the astronauts' lives might be saved. They prayed in factories across our land. The Chicago Board of Trade stopped trading—the ticker stopped. The customers and the brokers had a moment of silent prayer for the rescue of the Apollo 13 astronauts. Congress thought it so important that during their session they issued a proclamation urging people to pray for the rescue of Apollo 13."

Churches in the United States and all over the world held special prayer meetings, asking God for the safe return of the Apollo 13 astronauts. Jerry even heard that a mission in Burma and Christians in Guyana, West Africa, were praying. Jerry watched coworkers bow their heads at mission control and pray. Like hundreds of thousands of wafting columns of incense ascending to the heavens, prayers from all over the globe were lifted up in hopes that God would spare the lives of these three brave men.

The most pressing problem the NASA personnel had to address was the air filtration system. There was plenty of oxygen in the lunar lander to sustain all three men on their journey back to Earth. The problem was that the air filtration system would not be able to keep up with the new demands. The carbon dioxide the astronauts breathed out would eventually overwhelm the filtration system, and they would suffocate.

NASA engineers determined that the astronauts would have to take the filters out of the command ship (which were square) and reconfigure them to fit into the filtration system in the lunar lander (which was designed for round filters). The old adage "You can't fit a square peg in a round hole" was the exact problem these NASA engineers faced.

Jerry recalls how the engineers confronted the dilemma head-on: "That evening they put out on a table everything on Apollo 13 that might help them solve this difficulty. They even put out the plastic bags they would've used for moon rocks—everything they knew was on board.

"One of the technicians looked at those unrelated items and in his mind he saw a way of making the hoses from the spacesuits and those bags for the moon rocks and some cardboard covers fit together in a way that might make the filters work. I believe this was an answer to all the prayers going up. This technician drew a picture of the configuration he had envisioned, and the team got busy figuring out a procedure for the astronauts to follow to make it happen." Miraculously, the new system worked!

Though they'd overcome their first major hurdle, precious time was ticking away. Hundreds of scientists and engineers frantically went to work trying to solve their next obstacle: the failing electrical system. The astronauts would have to use the cone section of the command ship to reenter Earth's atmosphere; however, they had used up all the battery power in the command vessel when the ship's electricity went out. This battery power was essential to the systems needed to make a reentry. Without it they would not be able to come home.

One brilliant engineer designed a way they could "jump-start" the batteries in the command capsule with a makeshift jumper cable. Jerry remembers the engineer had to determine whether there was a piece of wire somewhere in the ship that would make his plan work.

"He wasn't even sure a suitable wire existed. But if he could find one, he would be able to connect the two power systems—the working one on the lunar lander and the one on the command ship with the depleted batteries. He could perhaps set the circuit breakers in such a configuration that he could trickle charge power through that wire into those depleted batteries in the reentry capsule."

After an intense search of the ship schematics, they found the necessary wire. The never-before-attempted procedure seemed workable, but it posed some risk. When they ran the procedure through computer simulations, the findings were not good. "The computer said, Don't use it; it's too dangerous," Jerry says. "But we had no other alternative. We had to do it, because without that power they couldn't reenter."

When the risky procedure was implemented, the computer warnings were correct. One of the battery cells literally exploded. "That was one of the most sobering moments of the return because it sounded just like another explosion, like the initial pop of that oxygen tank.

"But the miracle of it was that people's prayers were answered. Even though that battery cell exploded, that battery delivered nominal power the rest of the mission. Can you imagine that? A rigged jumper cable and an exploded battery and still everything works fine and those reentry batteries get recharged."

The final challenge was how to get the men back home. With the main rocket area on the command ship damaged, the engineers had to figure out a way to use the propulsion system on the lunar lander.

"That engine had never been intended to bring the whole craft back. It was just designed to go down to the moon's surface and then take off again. Now we were going to ask it to actually propel the entire assemblage of the lunar lander and the command ship around the moon and back to Earth." With time dangerously limited, hundreds of engineers and flight controllers worked tirelessly with the Apollo 13 astronauts to set up a step-by-step procedure to utilize the lunar lander's engine.

Jerry remembers being amazed at how these seemingly insurmountable obstacles fell away one by one. Plus, as Warning System Engineer, he knew how many things *didn't* go wrong that could have. For example, the explosion happened at just the right time. "Had it happened on the moon, or on the way back to Earth, or even much earlier in the mission, frankly we could not have saved those men. In fact, it even could've happened on the launch pad. Could you imagine the conflagration and devastation if the entire launch tower had exploded and burned to the ground? It would've ended the interest in manned space exploration for a number of years."

It just so happened that when the explosion occurred, one of the astronauts had just entered the lunar module and powered up some key systems. Because the hatch was open and the systems were powered up, the critical transition to their "lifeboat" was made much more quickly. It just seemed that at every step key elements were in place to help those men get back home.

As the troubled spacecraft approached Earth, there was one more dramatic twist: A hurricane loomed near the projected landing site in the Pacific Ocean. But as Apollo 13 prepared for reentry, the massive storm moved away from the splashdown area.

Of course, our three brave Apollo 13 astronauts did make it back. Amazingly, they landed at the projected splashdown coordinates with pinpoint accuracy despite all those major obstacles.

Before this adventure, Jerry had always compared spaceflight to a three-legged stool. One leg is the engineers who designed the spacecraft, one is the astronauts who flew it, and the third is the flight controllers who controlled their performance during missions. While he freely acknowledges the great courage of the Apollo 13 astronauts and the brilliance of the flight controllers and engineering team, he feels something was missing from his analogy: "For the Apollo 13 mission there had to be the fourth leg—God and answered prayer."

By the way, during his involvement with this historic Apollo lunar mission, Jerry Woodfill was not a Christian. But after seeing all that happened, how these men miraculously made it back to Earth, and how so many people all over the world had been praying, Jerry accepted Jesus Christ into his heart at a Christian Businessmen's Meeting.

"What can you say when you've seen these things happen firsthand? I was an eyewitness to every one of these events. I thought, if God could do the miracle of bringing men back from deep space that looked like they were lost, then He could reach down from that same mission control center in the heavens and give me guidance for my life."

If you'd like to learn more about Jerry's story, go to:
www.spaceacts.com.

JOY CLARK
No Ray of Light

I was locked up in houses where I was beaten with chairs.
I had guns to my head. A knife to the throat.
That's just typical for when you're a crack user and
you're out on the street.

Life in any big city can be exhilarating. The bright neon
signs seem to light up the night with excitement, and
there's always something going on. But for many, life
in the big city is ugly and sinister. For some, the dark angel of
crack cocaine lurks in the shadows and the alleyways, ready to
imprison all those who fall into his trap.

Joy Clark lived the dark life of a crack addict. For days,
sometimes weeks, she lived on the gray streets of Detroit trying
to scrape up enough money for her next fix. She'd get the
money any way she could. She would sell anything, sometimes
even herself.

"Crack cocaine to me is like Satan in the rawest form," she

says. "It takes everything away from people and they don't even know it. You just stand there in this cloud and you just don't know."

Her drug addictions started out innocently enough: by drinking socially in high school. Over the next ten years the occasional drink became a nightly event. Then the drinking dovetailed into cocaine use, and then the cocaine was replaced by crack.

"It starts as just a little tiny pea, basically, and then it just rolls and rolls. You don't realize what's happening until it becomes this big snowball. By the time I got to the end of it I was dumbfounded that it had gotten so bad."

When Joy married Michael Clark she already had two children from a previous marriage, James and Amanda. In that time it was like she had two lives. She'd live at home with her husband and children for a while. But then she'd get strung out on crack and live on the streets, sometimes for weeks at a time. Then she would check into a treatment program and get cleaned up and return to her family, only to be pulled back in by the drugs. She was trapped in this recurring cycle.

Joy's days as a drug addict on the streets of Detroit were dark and dangerous. "It was horrible. It was a living hell. I was locked up in houses where I was beaten with chairs. I had guns to my head. A knife to the throat. That's just typical for when you're a crack user and you're out on the street because that's the kind of people you are dealing with. It was like I was in this dark tunnel. And I would look and there would never be a ray of light."

She remembers running into a friend on the streets one cold night. Both of them had gone through rehab, and both thought the cycle might be broken. "We had both gotten clean. It was so ironic. Here it was only two months later and we ended up in the same crack house on the same night for the very first time back out there. We looked at each other and we went, 'What are we doing here? We know better.' The next day, they found her body in a dumpster."

Even with this sobering event, Joy could not break free from the crack that enslaved her. The statistics were not in her favor: Only one out of every one hundred crack users recovers to live a normal life. Officials had warned Joy that within three years she would either be dead, in jail, or committed to a mental institution. Since she had been a crack addict for five years, she knew she was living on borrowed time.

The problem with crack is that no matter how long you are clean, the next time you take it you immediately go back to the same level of addiction as before. "And so you mess up and you go back to it just one more time," Joy says. "The problem is that you don't start all over again; you start exactly where you left off."

Joy says that each time you take the drug your level of euphoria goes to higher and higher levels, but that is balanced by the fact that each time you come down off the drug, the crack takes you to the same intensity in the other direction. Each time the low point is progressively more unbearable, a stage or two worse than the time before. She says you would do anything—anything—to make the pain stop.

After each relapse or rehab session, Joy would vow to never do it again. She would be sober for days, weeks, even months at a time. But then one day the dark pull of the drugs would become overwhelming, and she would leave.

Her young children would cry at the front window of their house as they watched their mother go to the car. It was as if they could sense what was about to happen. "I can still see three-year-old Amanda's face begging, 'Mommy, please don't go.' Then I'd say, 'Oh, honey, I'm just going to get your French fries. I'll be right back, I promise.'" But it was a lie.

Joy says it was like being caught in a hamster's exercise wheel. "You run and run and you try to find a way out, but there is no way out. You just keep going in that same circle. It was like this dark pit and I was at the bottom of it. I would climb as hard as I could and dig my nails. My hands would be scarred, as I would try to climb up this pit to even see just a ray of light. But I would keep sliding back down no matter how hard I climbed or how far up I got. There was never any light."

But then one Easter, when Amanda was six, Joy's life hit rock bottom. She had been clean for a good while, but the demonic voice of crack put twisted thoughts into her head. She decided to take her little girl's Easter dress back to the store so she could get money for drugs. Joy remembers saying, "Honey, I've got to take the dress back. Mommy will get you another one. We'll be okay." But Joy didn't stop there. Next she took back little Amanda's Easter shoes. Her craving for crack heightened to the point that she needed to sell anything else she could.

Then came the last straw. "While Amanda was listening to her little kids' praise tape in my car stereo, I drove to the pawnshop to sell the stereo. I said, 'Mandy, I'm going to leave it here for a little while. I'll come back. We'll have it back soon.' Amanda crawled over the seat to the back of the car and just started crying, saying, 'Mommy, no, please. That's all I have left. Don't take it.' But I pawned that stereo with her little tape in it. She cried herself to sleep in the backseat. And that was it."

Joy dropped Mandy off with a relative to go on her crack binge. When it was over, she came home just like she had done so many times before. But this time the house was empty. Michael was gone, and he had taken the children with him. He had packed up almost all of their belongings and taken them. He didn't want to leave anything of value that Joy could use to get more drugs.

She was stunned. She stood crying in the hollow shell of a house. The walls and the floors were bare. The home was virtually empty. There were no sounds of little children's feet running in the hallway. No little laughing faces. Just emptiness. Joy had never felt so broken and alone.

But it was Easter Sunday, 1993—a day for miraculous rebirth. Sometimes it takes a death of sorts to wake us up to new life. God began doing a miracle inside of Joy's heart that day. You see, Joy had a God-fearing mother who had been praying for her for years, who had spent many sleepless nights pleading with the Lord on behalf of her daughter. Michael was also praying for his wife's recovery. Hundreds of people at their local church had been praying.

In her brokenness, Joy got down on her knees and prayed. "I said, 'Lord, I can't do it no more.' And it was over. I think He knows when we're at our edge. He knows when we mean what we say. And I told Him, 'It's either the crack or my life. You've got to take one or the other because I can't do it anymore.' And that's the day He delivered me."

Joy has never gone back to the crack. She'd been to inpatient and outpatient programs, twelve-step programs, and self-help groups for years. But it was her heartfelt prayer that morning that was the only remedy that could heal her completely. "It was awesome. I mean, I spent ten years of fighting it, in and out of treatments, going through all the different programs, but nothing worked. And then, in just one moment, He took it away—and it was gone!"

God was not done with Joy. Her lifestyle on the streets of Detroit had taken its toll on her body. Joy had PID, a sexually transmitted disease that damages a woman's reproductive system. A year after the Lord gave her victory over crack, she began longing to have a child with her husband, Michael. But PID all but ruled that out.

Joy remembers the horrible medical news. "The doctors told us, 'She's not having a baby. Give it up. We've done the tests. Her tubes are blocked. They're so bad we can't even repair them. Unless you have fifteen thousand dollars to do artificial insemination, it's not going to happen.'" Michael and Joy were crushed. They didn't have the money for artificial insemination. Having another child appeared to be a lost cause.

But God is in the business of performing the impossible.

To the doctor's amazement, Joy got pregnant—not once, but twice! Joy has given birth to two more children since 1995: Bethany and Hannah. She calls them her miracle babies.

Joy remembers something she heard her mother say once. "This court worker looked at my mom and told her, 'Listen, this girl—her statistics are low. Give up the hope. She will never be nothing but a crack addict. I deal with these every day. Just give it up.' And my mom said, 'Absolutely not. You don't know the God that I know. And I know He will take care of her. He will bring her home.'"

And He did bring Joy home on that glorious Easter morning. Joy says God spoke these words to her heart: "Joy, when I delivered you, I threw your sin as far as the east is from the west. I buried it in the deepest sea as if it never was. Because when I say it's gone, it's gone."

CORNEL POTRA
A Quest for Freedom

All of a sudden the door burst open and
several officers with machine guns flooded the room....
They confiscated the Bibles, hymnbooks, and
anything else they considered to be religious....
And then they began to write down names.

In my travels as a reporter there are some things you see that you never forget. I was in Romania in the early 1990s. Communism had fallen, and the country was starting to heal spiritually. I was assigned to help produce a children's gospel special that was being shot in the gorgeous Transylvanian Alps.

One day as we were driving to our shooting location, I noticed a large, concrete, boxlike structure at the side of the road. When I looked at it, something in my soul felt it was evil. The structure was bleak looking, standing about two stories tall, with steps on the side leading up to a platform area. As we traveled down this country road, I saw these platforms every twenty miles or so. I asked my translator what they were.

He explained to me that during the communist rule in Romania these platforms were staffed with military personnel equipped with binoculars. They took down the license plate number of every car that passed. The eyes of the government were always following you.

His explanation sent chills down my American spine. I couldn't envision a government having that much control in my life. Imagine a haunting world of deep spiritual darkness, a world where you cannot freely talk about your faith in Jesus Christ. Imagine that because of your faith you would not be allowed to attend college or have a professional career.

Imagine a world where policemen could storm into your home and confiscate your Bible, where you had to meet in secrecy with the windows covered so your neighbors couldn't see that you were having a prayer meeting. And if you ever decided to talk publicly about your faith, you ran the risk of being interrogated, beaten, imprisoned, and even sent off to a mental institution.

This is the world that Cornel Potra faced every day.

Cornel became a Christian at the age of fourteen. He and his nine brothers and sisters grew up in a loving Christian home in the city of Oradia in Romania. His father worked construction and served as a leader in their church.

When school officials found out that Cornel was a Christian, they made him a public example to the other students. He recalls the pain he felt as a young boy: "When my teachers found out that I was a Christian, they asked me to stand before the class and give an account of how I spent my Sundays. I told them I went to church. The students were encouraged to make fun of me and even to beat up on me. And the teachers lowered my grades many times."

Cornel says that groups of teachers would hold private sessions to encourage him to change his beliefs. "I remember being called in before all the teachers in the school and being humiliated. They asked me not to go to church anymore. Actually they organized these atheistic meetings on Sundays for the Christian students so that they would not go to church but instead go to school and be indoctrinated with evolutionism and atheism."

Needless to say, Cornel's high school years were not easy. And when he graduated he knew he would be denied access to the University of Romania because of his faith.

Those who did move on to higher education were under intense pressure to join the Communist Party. If they refused, the government did not look kindly on their careers. When job assignments were given out, nonparty members were sent far away from their hometowns and loved ones. If professionals became Christians, often they were demoted or fired.

Occasionally government officials would call a citizen in. Many times these became life-or-death situations. Cornel recalls, "It depended on what kind of activity that person was involved in. If the security people considered an individual to be a dangerous element, such as a religious person who had influence over others, then he was marked as a traitor to the system and called in for interrogation. Some would be beaten so severely they would die. People would simply never hear from them again. Others would be sent to work in labor camps far away from their families."

At times, Cornel was involved in the dangerous practice of Bible smuggling. His home was near the Hungarian border and he had a mastery of English. He became a valuable asset to foreign missionaries who wanted to smuggle the Word in.

"Bibles were very scarce in Romania," Cornel remembers. "People would copy it by hand and pass it on to others. They would use carbon copy paper to copy Bible verses and pass them on. The distribution of whole Bibles in Romania was done very secretly. Many times the Bibles were caught and the people who handled them were put in jail, beaten up, tortured, mistreated—along with their families."

Even though government churches did exist, Cornel attended unofficial church meetings. Each Monday, pastors from the official churches had to report all activity at their churches. Police wanted to know key information, such as who had attended the services that weekend.

Cornel would walk for miles into the country to attend an underground prayer meeting. The family hosting the service lived outside the city limits. They blocked and sealed the windows so no one could see the activity inside the house. Still, a neighbor called the police.

"One night as we were praying, all of a sudden the door burst open and several officers with machine guns flooded the room. They pointed their machine guns at us and told us to stand up." Yelling at the frightened group, the officers confiscated the Bibles, hymnbooks, and anything else they considered religious and therefore dangerous to society. And then they began to write down names. "They wanted to take us all to the police station, but we were too many to fit in their police van. So they just took our names."

School officials confronted Cornel the next day. "They called me before all the teachers in the school and shamed me. How dare I spend my evening going to a prayer meeting instead of studying? At that time my grades were okay, but after that they were lowered. The teachers said it would give me more reason to stay home and study instead of wasting my time in prayer meetings."

Cornel realized his future in Romania was bleak. He longed for life in a country where he could worship God and read his Bible without the fear of government intervention. He tried several times to escape. The first time he was caught an officer beat Cornel until he signed an incriminating statement. His parents were given a hefty fine.

Following his next failed escape attempt in August of 1985, he was jailed in Hungary for thirty days and then sentenced to forced labor in Romania for a full year.

If he tried again, Cornel knew his punishment could mean death or banishment to a mental hospital. But he had to try again. Cornel felt he had no other choice: His desire to worship God freely burned in his heart. So in 1988 he tried to escape one more time. Cornel and a Christian brother made their way by rail to a small village on the Romanian-Yugoslavian border.

Their journey took a dangerous turn when they got off the train. Cornel explains, "It was risky there. Since the village was close to the border, soldiers checked the IDs of everyone who got off the train. Most of the officers and border guards would know the local people by sight. Through a miracle of God they did not ID me."

With danger lurking on every street corner, Cornel and his friend made it to a safe house. His companion had relatives in the village who were aiding them in their escape attempt. Early the next morning the two men disguised themselves as local workers and headed out.

"We took a couple of bikes and rode into the field. All workers had to go by a watchtower where they were ID'd and allowed to go work in the field. So we went into a cornfield and waited for my friend's relatives to signal us when the border guards were changing shifts."

There would be a critically short amount of time, just moments, as the guards changed places at their border posts. Many people had died making a mad dash for the border across this narrow strip of sandy ground. Those who were shot attempting to escape were buried on the spot. This dark knowledge haunted Cornel's mind.

"My friend's relatives whistled. That was the signal. But my friend was too scared to go. We prayed together and finally we ran across the border into Yugoslavia."

But they weren't out of danger yet. If the Yugoslav guards caught them, they would be sent back to Romania. News of the two young men's escape made it to the border guards in Yugoslavia, but Cornel and his friend miraculously dodged their pursuers.

Within days they made it almost to the Austrian border. But as they walked in the cold darkness, something unthinkable was about to happen. Cornel remembers, "As we were walking through the woods, my friend, being a heavyset man, fell and made some noise. The Yugoslavian border guards shot bullets in the air and came with dogs. We were both hidden in the bushes, but my friend was so afraid that he turned himself in."

Cornel stayed hidden, but the soldiers seemed to sense that someone else was still in the woods. Cornel remained motionless for what seemed like hours. He felt that if he was caught it would mean certain death.

"The soldiers were looking for me for quite some time. It was five o'clock in the morning when one Yugoslavian border guard was standing by the bush where I was and my watch beeped. But the Lord must've just deafened him—that border guard did not hear it! Another soldier came and flashed his light right on me, but the Lord blinded him and he did not see me. Because of these miracles I was able to crawl into another cornfield close by and then escape into Austria. Another friend met me there.

"I went to a refugee camp close to Vienna where I spent about ten months. In the meantime I applied for political asylum in the United States of America. After ten and a half months I was granted asylum and allowed to come to the States."

Cornel arrived at John F. Kennedy Airport in New York on June 13, 1989. His newfound religious freedom in the United States was a source of extreme joy. But that joy was dampened when he learned that within months of his own escape, his younger brother, Abraham, had been killed immediately after crossing the Austrian border. With all freedom there is a cost. Cornel's family paid that cost with the ultimate sacrifice.

Cornel's new life in America has been miraculous. He married a young Romanian woman who had come to the United States at the age of twelve. They've been blessed with three beautiful children. Cornel graduated from Bible college then law school. He recently passed his bar exam and has worked extensively with the American Center for Law and Justice. There he helped prepare argued cases defending the religious freedom of Americans. He's also been instrumental in defending religious rights cases in Europe.

Cornel is truly living his dream. All of his immediate family now live in America, too. "I am so thankful to God for my family. I am thankful to the Lord for my mother and father who prayed for me. I am thankful to God for the freedom that I had in this country to continue with a good education and for the doors God opened for me. And I am thankful to God because I am alive. It is an exciting time in history to serve the Lord."

PATTI AND ADRIANNE WEBSTER

The Day the Shots Rang Out

All of a sudden I just felt something hit me in the back.
Of course, I'd never been shot before. It hurt so much.
I screamed so loud.

It was a hot morning on June 18, 1993. A light summer shower had washed away some of the oppressive heat that had been hanging in the air that day.

That morning Patti Webster was in her charming single-story home on a tree-lined street in a normally quiet neighborhood in Bryan, Texas. Her husband, Bob, was at work at the local cable company. Their twenty-three-year-old son, Jeremy, was asleep in his bedroom, and Adrianne, their thirteen-year-old daughter, was playing outside in the front yard with her fifteen-year-old friend, Anna.

The girls were splashing around in the puddles in the front yard, unaware that tragedy was about to strike, unaware that a dark force was about to shatter their lives forever. Anna had recently broken up with her twenty-year-old boyfriend, Joe, who lived just up the street. Joe wanted revenge. In an evil fit of anger, he decided to kill Anna and anyone that stood in his way. He took a semiautomatic rifle, wrapped it in a towel, and headed down the street to where Adrianne and Anna were playing.

"I saw Joe come out of his house and this really strange feeling came over me, this real dread," Adrianne says. "I didn't see the gun in his hand because he had it wrapped up in that towel. All of a sudden I just felt something hit me in the back. Of course, I'd never been shot before. It hurt so much. I screamed so loud that my mom heard me. I imagine all the neighbors heard me."

Adrianne watched in horror as the small bloodstain widened at her waist. Patti came out and saw what was happening. She immediately got the girls into the house and ran to dial 9-1-1 as Joe stepped up on the porch and headed for the front door. Jeremy heard his sister's screams and bolted from his bedroom. He made it to the living room just in time to throw all of his weight on the front door and lock it shut.

Joe began to shoot wildly. He shot out windows—broken glass rained down on the living room floor. More shots rang out as he moved along the side of the house to the back door.

Jeremy pulled Anna into the bathroom and tried to calm her down. Adrianne ran into her bedroom and locked the door. Patti was in the back portion of the house, right by the back door, frantically talking to the 9-1-1 operator.

Everyone thought the back door was locked, but it wasn't. Joe simply opened the door and stood face-to-face with Patti. Frozen in fear, Patti watched Joe raise his gun and walk slowly toward her. His eyes were glazed over. His movements were robotic and unnatural. He was mumbling incoherently that nobody loved him, no one wanted to be his friend.

"He shot me four times," Patti says. "Twice in the chest and once in each arm. And that is when I fell down. I must have passed out for a minute because I don't remember falling, but I remember opening my eyes. I was lying on the floor."

When Patti came to, the muzzle of Joe's gun was pointed right at her face. "He was just standing there. I thought, he's either going to kill me or he's going to shoot me in the head and I'll be brain dead." Though badly injured, she still wanted to stay alive. Knowing that if she didn't act quickly she would be dead, she used her right foot to smash the gun against the door frame.

As soon as Jeremy realized Joe had made it into the house, he flew to his mother's aid. Both he and Patti struggled to wrestle the weapon out of Joe's hands.

Then Joe's attack took a strange turn. It was as if Joe began to realize what he was doing. "He was moving the gun like we weren't even holding onto it," Patti says. "We just had no effect on him. But then he took that gun with us hanging onto it and put it in his mouth. He was going to kill himself right there. I thought, well, if he shoots himself then he can't hurt anybody else."

But during the struggle Jeremy's thumb got lodged behind the trigger. Joe couldn't fire the gun. Then Patti blurted out a shocking statement. "What came out of my mouth was, 'Joe, you'll just go to hell!' He could not pull the trigger because Jeremy's thumb was in the way. And then he just let go of the gun."

Once they finally got the gun out of Joe's hands, Patti called Adrianne and Anna out of their rooms and onto the porch. Joe collapsed and sat down on the floor. His clothes were covered with Patti's blood.

Adrianne remembers the sickening fear she felt when she saw Joe outside her doorway. "I was still screaming. Anna knocked on my door and yelled, 'Adrianne, it's okay. It's over.' So I finally opened the door. Joe was slumped down on the floor right in front of my door. That freaked me out. I walked around to the side. I followed the trail of blood all the way out to the porch. I saw that the front window was broken out. I just went and sat on the front porch swing and waited there."

Within minutes, police and emergency medical personnel arrived on the scene. Patti sat on the front porch in shock, her clothes terribly bloodied. Police had to convince her that everything was all right before she would release Joe's gun from her desperate grip. Their entire ordeal had lasted less than fifteen minutes.

Patti and Adrianne were rushed to the hospital. Bob got an emergency call at work and met them there. They soon found out how lucky they had been. If their wounds had been off by mere inches, both Adrianne and Patti would have suffered major complications.

"With Adrianne, I think the shot was only an inch from her spine," Patti recalls. "They said that if she had been shot any closer to her spine, she could've been paralyzed for life. The bullet went straight through—her wound didn't bleed much at all. She was released from the hospital the very next morning. That was a miracle."

Patti felt she was protected in an amazing way, too. "I was

shot in both arms: one shot in the wrist and the other one in the forearm. Both bullets went straight through without hitting bone. The first thing the paramedics asked me was whether I could move my hands. They said that the wounds I received should've damaged the nerves so severely that I wouldn't be able to use my hands. But my hands were fine."

She had also been shot twice in the chest. "I had been facing Joe at an angle. The first bullet went right past the breastbone into the left lung. If I had been facing him, it would've gone right into my heart and I would've been dead. Another shot went in the left shoulder at an angle and came out under my arm. I have no permanent injuries at all. I didn't have a great loss of blood. There was no operation. They didn't even give me a transfusion."

Like any typical father, Patti's husband, Bob, felt regret that he had not been there to protect his family. For days he felt a deep sense of guilt. "I went into a numb mental state of not really being able to function. My family tells me I was useless for about a week. Places I was used to going—I'd get lost driving to them. It was like being in the twilight zone.

"I think the only thing that helped me through my anger about not being there to protect them was that God protected them so well. Not only did God preserve Patti's and Adrianne's and Anna's and Jeremy's lives, but Joe's also. And who knows what would've happened if I *had* been there? That is how I came to a peace about not being there."

To everyone's amazement, Bob and Patti Webster say they've forgiven Joe. In fact, they have written him several times in prison. When they found out that Joe had accepted Jesus Christ as his Savior, they were thrilled.

But some people did not understand the Websters' attitude toward Joe. "Individuals would say, 'Let me have ten minutes with him,'" Bob recalls. "'The court won't have to spend or waste any money because I will go ahead and eliminate him.' I would respond, 'I'm sorry you feel that way. God's in control of this whole thing. I don't have any hatred for that man.'

"When Jesus was crucified, He didn't vent hatred on anybody, even though they were doing Him wrong. He said, 'Father, forgive them; they don't know what they are doing.' That is what I have felt for Joe."

The Websters knew what Joe had been through growing up. "When he was a young boy," Bob says, "he saw his dad get killed—shot to death. His little brother is in prison now, too, serving life without parole for killing a man in a random drive-by shooting. We used to invite Joe and other kids in the neighborhood into our home. We had cake with them. We took them to church and things like that."

Both Bob and Patti feel they've learned a tremendous lesson from this ordeal. "As much as you love your kids and you don't want them to suffer," Patti says, "in the end you have to trust God to watch over them.

"We protected our kids as much as we could from being exposed to anything that could hurt them. I was always playing with them, being with them, watching over them. I tried to protect them from things that might hurt them. I always had to know where Adrianne was going, and she had to call when she got there. We checked out places before she went to make sure everything was okay.

"But when this happened, I realized that some things are out of your control. You can't protect your children perfectly. If they are going to be protected, God's going to have to protect them. You have to trust God to take care of your kids."

THE McLEAN FAMILY
The Light in the Darkness

I saw that the sun was going down on the horizon....
I looked back but couldn't see any of the trail.
Then I knew we really were in a precarious situation.

Each of us makes hundreds of small, seemingly insignificant decisions every day. We choose between sleeping in on a Saturday morning or getting up early to go for a jog. We choose either to take a bag lunch to work or to go out to eat with friends. But sometimes our routine decisions can bring about major life-changing events.

On Christmas Day 1989, Pastor George McLean and his wife, Sonya, made what appeared to be a minor decision: They elected to celebrate the holiday by taking the family cross-country skiing. So George and Sonya, their sons, Mark and David, and two of their friends took off to the gorgeous Laurel Mountains of Pennsylvania.

Almost every ski shop was closed that Christmas morning,

but they finally found one that was open. The kind man at the shop fitted the family with the correct equipment and then told them where to get a map of the cross-country ski trails in the area. When they arrived at the ranger station to pick up the map, it was closed. But they spotted a trail entrance nearby. Figuring the trail would run only a couple of miles and ultimately return them to the highway, they strapped on their skis and plunged ahead.

George McLean remembers the beauty of that day. "It was really an enjoyable experience. After we got acclimated to the skis, we really moved along. We got far back into the pine forest. The snow and trees and all were just incredibly beautiful. We were really enjoying it and singing Christmas carols together. It was truly—in fact, we sang it—a winter wonderland."

But their fun family outing soon turned dangerous. The McLeans didn't realize it yet, but they were on a system of trails that was seventy miles long and reached some of the highest elevations in that region of Pennsylvania. "We were in an area that was extremely secluded. I guess the one big danger that we weren't even aware of at the time was that there was no one else anywhere around because it was Christmas Day."

Snow began to fall heavily. Pastor McLean realized that he couldn't see the trail very well and that their own tracks were quickly disappearing under the snow. With no way to go forward and no way to go back, they would be completely lost. It finally hit him that his family was in trouble.

"I just got this incredibly anxious feeling when I looked up and saw that the sun was going down on the horizon. I looked back but couldn't see any of the trail. Then I knew we really were going to be in a precarious situation if we couldn't find our way out and find it pretty soon."

Their younger son, David, recalls the brutal conditions that descended upon them at sundown. "It was extremely cold. The wind chill was way below zero. We had been out there for quite a few hours at that point. The sun had gone down. The wind was blowing fiercely. The snow was coming down. We weren't properly attired: We were wearing jeans, but the jeans had gotten wet and had frozen. I remember the cold and the damp went through your coat and your pants and your clothing. It just went right through it. There was no way to get out of the weather."

The long hours in the freezing cold began to take their toll. Signs of frostbite started to set in. The pain was minimal while they were moving, but the moment they stopped and then tried to move forward again, the pain would be unbearable.

"It was just unbelievable to realize that we were in a situation that was life threatening, yet there was nothing we could do," Sonya says. "Without some kind of intervention, there was absolutely no way we were going to get out of there. At one point I think I became really sort of hysterical. I was crying. Just absolutely crying. I remember experiencing unbelievable pain. Then I began feeling numb. What I really wanted to do was stop and just shut my eyes and rest. I think that's probably the worst thing you can do."

As their ordeal continued late into the night, George made a difficult decision. He decided that they should stop, hold their ground, and hope for someone to come rescue them. When they stopped, David found something rather surprising in his wet clothes. "I'd actually forgotten that I had these matches in my jacket. I pulled everything out of that pocket—everything else was wet except the matches."

David's find gave the family new hope. They decided to try to build a signal fire. "The snow was really coming down," George recalls. "Every time we would strike a match and get it down to the kindling on the rocks, the match would go out. We'd try again, and it would go out again. We did that for two or three hours.

"I would go digging through the snow, falling down in it, trying to find something that was dry and might burn. Occasionally we might find a little stick or something that we thought might be able to start the fire. We brought it back and would try, but it was all futility."

Finally, George gave up. After hours of trying to build the fire in the cold and the wet and the snow, he began to think it was impossible. But Sonya urged her husband to try one more time. Pastor McLean launched one last attempt. "We found a few little leaves buried under some snow. I clutched those in my hands, covered them up, and made my way back. We put those down and I asked if anybody had anything to add to it.

"The fellas took out their billfolds. If we had anything that was paper—season passes, coupons, gift certificates, anything—we pulled it out." Their son Mark even tore off a corner of his social security card. Their friend Kevin took out a picture of his deceased wife. He looked at her face for several moments and then tore the photo into small pieces, quietly placing them on their little pile of kindling.

They were down to only a few matches. They prayed together, asking God for a miracle. George lifted his face to the night sky. Something felt different. It took him a moment to realize that he didn't feel snow falling on his face.

They carefully struck one of their last matches. Cupping their hands to shield that small flame of hope against the freezing wind, they slowly moved the flame to the frail pile of paper and leaves. That small orange flame began to flicker over the meager mound of paper. Miraculously their tiny fire began to grow!

With renewed vigor the entire family took turns running into the dark forest to find more food for the fire. "I remember very vividly reaching down into the snow trying to find any kind of limbs or leaves that we could try to burn," Mark says. "It was so dark. I remember trying to do that in total darkness." In the race to feed the fire, Sonya fell and was injured.

But they stayed at it and finally their persistence paid off: They heard a faint sound in the distance. "We heard this sound and it seemed to get louder," George says. "Our hearts were just kind of leaping, thinking there was somebody out there looking for us. It got closer, but we still couldn't see anything. It was just pitch black.

"Then all of a sudden right out of that dark forest we saw a light coming—a forest ranger on a snowmobile. We yelled to get his attention. They'd been searching for us. Out of about eight trails they were going to search, we were on the next to the last one. They couldn't believe we were able to get back so far." The McLeans had been in the subzero weather for almost thirteen hours.

Due to her injuries, Sonya was taken out of the forest first. When she made it to the makeshift emergency area, medical professionals were ready. "I was absolutely freezing. They just put blankets and blankets on me. They massaged my feet.

They gave me candy bars to eat. They gave me orange juice—anything they could to help the situation."

Later, after the rest of their party had been safely retrieved, one of the rescue workers approached Sonya with a remarkable statement. "A park ranger said to me, 'We were talking among ourselves, and we think that even with our experience none of us could have gotten a fire started tonight.' At that point I knew that God had given us a miracle."

To the McLeans, that snowmobile's headlight cutting through the oppressive darkness was a powerful symbol. "The light not only meant that we were going to be rescued," David says, "it also meant hope. Just seeing that light in the middle of the darkness was very intense. We knew that if we'd had to be out there too much longer we were not going to survive. That light gave us the sense that everything was going to be all right. That the storm had passed. We forgot about the pain. We forgot about how really cold we were. We were filled with joy and gratitude and warmth."

Pastor George McLean says their dramatic rescue has totally refocused his view of the holidays. "All of this has made Christmas much more meaningful for us. When I saw that light coming through and heard that engine, I thought to myself, What joy Christ is in the midst of our darkness and sin. People are lost and don't know the way to go, but then the light of the world comes shining in."

CAROLYN DENISE KEMP

Crying in the Moonlight

Our first night in the homeless shelter was scary.
A lot of the people in there were from mental institutions....
They would be screaming at the air and throwing things—
just crazy stuff.

Thousands of women face the unthinkable every day. Some face physical or mental abuse; some fear for the lives of their children. Pushed beyond all rational limits, they must flee abusive and dangerous situations.

Carolyn Denise Kemp knew in her heart it was time to take her two boys and escape. For a good while, Carolyn thought maybe she could correct the problems. But ultimately she realized that no matter what she did, the situation worsened. Finally, with no place to go, without a friend to turn to, she fled with O. J., age eleven, and Christopher, age seven. She had to find a better life for her boys.

Frightened and confused, Carolyn and her two boys left

their beautiful, three-bedroom Florida home and pool and set off on their quest. She didn't know exactly where she was going, but she went. She drove for hours until her car finally came to rest in central Florida. The three tired travelers got the last room at the homeless shelter in Orlando.

"It was very hard for me," Carolyn says. "There were times when I would sit in the bathroom and just cry. I felt angry and then sometimes I felt hurt. You look at your kids and you think—Why are my kids in this situation? What happened in our lives that would bring us down this far?

"When people would ask me, 'Why Orlando?' I would say, 'I don't know why.' The only thing I could tell them was that I was just directed there. I had never done anything like that in my life."

Though they were thankful to get the last room in the shelter, their new living quarters were like a strange nightmare. "Our first night in the homeless shelter was scary. A lot of the people in there were from mental institutions. You had to be very, very careful. They would be walking up and down the hall talking to themselves. They would be screaming at the air and throwing things—just crazy stuff. It scared Christopher, my youngest one, a lot. And that was hard for me. So I made sure I stayed very close to them. I had to keep myself together because I had a seven-year-old and an eleven-year-old."

Carolyn had been used to making her own decisions for herself and the boys. But in the shelter, those decisions were made for her. "Everybody had to be out of the shelter by ten-thirty in the morning. You weren't allowed to come back inside until four-thirty that afternoon. So if you didn't have a job, you just wandered the hot streets of Orlando until you found one. You had to make sure you showered before you came to dinner. You had to bring your wet towels down with you. They gave you this little ticket to go in and get dinner. You had to be in bed by eight-thirty. All the lights were out by nine o'clock."

The long nights were filled with explosive screams and intense arguments outside their quiet room. But since they weren't allowed to close their bedroom door all the way, privacy was limited.

Carolyn, constantly worried about her children's emotional welfare, vowed to do whatever was necessary to get her boys out of that shelter as soon as possible. Even before her initial interviews in the shelter were completed, she'd already started an intense job search.

Carolyn remembers getting angry during some of her interviews. She was a well-educated woman, but when people saw her homeless shelter address, they presupposed she was ignorant. One man took away the pen and some forms Carolyn was about to fill out, assuming she was illiterate. Another interviewer started talking to Carolyn as if she were deaf. "I asked him something and he started speaking real loud and slow, trying to make sure I understood every word."

To make their stay in the shelter as short as possible, Carolyn worked two jobs, one during the day and one at night. The worst thing about it, though, was not the grueling work schedule but leaving her two boys alone. "It was extremely hard to have to leave them. I saw those people during the day at the shelter; I knew what was going on. I knew there were only one or two staff members there at any time. And with forty to fifty families, I knew they couldn't always be watching out for my boys. So to leave them there at night to go to work was really the hardest thing."

Unbeknownst to Carolyn, Christopher would cry himself to sleep every night. O. J. would crawl into his bed and put his arms around him. In the darkness he would whisper in Christopher's ear that everything was going to be okay.

As the moonlight glistened on the oil-stained pavement of the convenience store parking lot, Carolyn would clean the outdoor pay phones with one hand and with the other clutch her heart. When no one was around in the early misty hours of the morning, she would let her tears fall and let her sobs cut into the still blackness of the night. Every time she left her boys alone, another piece of her heart would break.

Other times Carolyn reflected on how belittled she felt as a person. People had no idea why she was in that shelter. They did not know the reasons she had to flee her normal life or why she ended up homeless. Some just came to the conclusion that anyone homeless must be stupid or just too lazy to pay the bills.

How could Carolyn's situation become worse? Well, one day when she came out of the shelter to go to work, she found that her car had been stolen. Carolyn needed that car to get her to work so she could get her family out of the homeless shelter. But the parking space outside the shelter was empty.

Most people would've sat down in that parking lot and screamed and cried and hit the ground with their fists. But Carolyn reached down inside of herself and held onto something in the deepest part of her soul. This woman had an unbelievable bedrock of faith in her heart that was amazing to everyone who knew her.

She was reminded of something she'd done when they first came to the shelter. She'd had Christopher lie down on the ground for her visual aid. "I said, 'This is where we are—at the bottom. But we have a choice. We can either stay down here or we can get up and fight and trust God.' And they said, 'Momma, we're gonna get up and fight.' So Christopher got up off the floor and we held hands and told God we were going to trust Him."

As she looked at that empty parking space, Carolyn sensed that God was already beginning to answer their prayers, but she had no idea about all of the doors God was soon to open for her children.

Weeks before, she'd had an idea: "While we were in the shelter I took some pictures of the boys in the park. Then I looked in the phone book and sent the pictures out to different talent agents. The Christensen Group called us. They liked the boys and signed them on the spot." Within days, Carolyn's sons had signed with one of the most respected talent agencies in the Orlando area.

Now, however, her car was gone. The thought came to her that this would prevent her boys from taking part in these wonderful opportunities. But after all she had been through with God, she believed He would not let such a thing happen. She was right. Carolyn borrowed friends' cars and used the public bus system to get her sons to auditions and talent jobs.

Soon her boys won roles with some of the biggest names in entertainment. O. J. got a part in a production at Walt Disney World. He also landed a regular spot as a "Student Adventurer" on the national educational show *Shamu TV,* being shot at Sea World. And Christopher starred in a commercial for the "Kids'

Choice Awards," shot at Nickelodeon Studios on Universal property.

Carolyn hadn't known why she'd ended up in Orlando when she left home, but God had known. He had clearly directed her to one of the only places on the East Coast where her sons would have a shot at landing unbelievable national talent jobs. It was all part of His plan of financial deliverance for her family.

Even though Carolyn had done her best as a working mother, the loss of the car and later her job were hard financial blows. Because of the miraculous provision God gave them through O. J.'s and Christopher's talent work, Carolyn and her sons were able to get out of the homeless shelter and stay out.

But looking back, the Kemps feel God was watching out for them during the whole ordeal. Carolyn felt that God not only protected her sons in the shelter but that He also made their room a place of peace and rest in the turmoil of that shelter. Many of the other children in the shelter came into their room to get away from the insanity of the residents. It was like a calm in the midst of a vast storm. Carolyn and the boys had tremendous times of praying and singing and Bible reading that seemed to quiet their own hearts and minds as well as those of the other children.

"I just can't imagine walking through all of that without the Lord," Carolyn says. "He watched over those boys. If you were to spend a night in the shelter, then you would understand the miracle of just that alone. I mean, you would stand in our room and you would hear nothing but chaos outside. And our room was so peaceful, just so anointed. God was so faithful."

But Carolyn also feels she learned a great deal about homelessness. "It helped me to understand that most people don't realize how close a number of folks are to being in the shelter. People in these shelters are not necessarily lazy or ignorant. There were a number of reasons why they were there. There was a nurse. There was a teacher there with four daughters."

Carolyn, O. J., and Christopher spent four months in the homeless shelter in Orlando. But when you talk to them today, there is not one ounce of bitterness concerning the hard time they went through there. Today O. J. is an honors student in college. He is still getting impressive auditions and jobs with major national clients. Christopher is now in high school in a specialized magnet program studying science.

When asked what the Lord means to her, Carolyn replies, "He just means the world to me. I asked Him to prove to me that He really is God, and He did. And for that I bless Him because I could never turn my back on Him. I know that He's ordaining and approving every single step I make. He's saying yes to it and He's allowing us to go to the next step. He is just totally, totally awesome."

REESE
⟋⟍
One Woman's Fight for Emotional Survival

*He had on a leather jacket and when he moved it back
I could see that he had a gun. Then he said,
"I really think you should get out of the car now."*

When I interviewed Reesee, I got angry—very angry. You meet a nice young woman like Reesee, and you see a life that was marred by the violent act of rape. You see a family that was broken. You can't imagine this ever happening to your daughter, wife, sister, or mother. You see the innocence that was totally ripped away from this young Christian woman, and you can't help but become furious. I can't even tell you her full name because there are still some ongoing issues connected with this story.

Reesee grew up in a strong Christian home in the Bible Belt. Her father was a traveling evangelist, and Reesee sang with a gospel group and worked extensively with the children's and women's ministries at her church.

Her tragedy began one day when she went shopping with her teenage cousin and her cousin's friend, both of whom were sixteen. Reesee was twenty-seven. The three came out of a store and saw two good-looking young men in the parking lot by Reesee's car.

"They were very clean-cut," Reesee recalls. "They looked like the kind of guys you could go to church with. Their hair was short. They were meticulously dressed. No facial hair. No mustaches. They were so neatly dressed in stylish leather jackets. They had a Jeep. They began to talk to us and tell the girls how cute they were."

The guys asked them to meet them at an outdoor park where a basketball game would be going on. "I thought, well, there's going to be parents there and there'll be adults there and coaches and stuff. So it'll be okay."

When they were at the park, Reesee and the girls stayed in the car while they talked to the two men. The younger of the two stood on the passenger side, joking with the teenage girls. Reesee remembers that they were having a wonderful time. The older man talked only to Reesee.

After a while the crowds started to thin out. That's when the older boy's conversation turned ugly.

"The guy on my side asked me to get out of the car and I refused. He had on a leather jacket and when he moved it back I could see that he had a gun. Then he said, 'I really think you should get out of the car now.'"

"I started to reach for the keys to start the car and he got real close to me. He said, 'Look, we can do this the easy way or the hard way. You get out of the car now and your friends will be all right. If you don't, you know, it's not a big deal. I'll kill you now. I'll kill you then. It does not matter. But if you don't do what I tell you, you will suffer the consequences and so will they.'"

Reesee's young companions could not hear what the man was saying to her. They were focused on the charming young man on their side.

"All I could think was that my cousin and her friend were just kids and I was responsible for them. I thought, If I do what he says then maybe he won't hurt the girls." Reesee got out of the car and went with the stranger. "When we got in the Jeep he pulled away from where the girls were. I thought, If he takes it out on me then maybe they'll be all right.

"The other guy stayed behind with them. 'You don't have to worry,' he told me in the Jeep. 'As long as you do what I tell you, they'll be fine. But if you don't and I give the signal then they are going to die.'

"I had no way of knowing if he was telling me the truth or not. I mean I was sitting in there with a man with a gun. I had no clue.

"He started to tell me to do things. I refused. He hit me once with his fist. I had never been hit in the face before in my entire life. Violence had never been a part of my life. I still refused. Then he pulled the gun and he told me that if I didn't do what he wanted he would kill me. I just couldn't do it. He was trying to kiss me and pull at my clothes. I started fighting him. Then he hit me in the temple with the gun and I don't remember anything else."

Moments later Reesee awakened—and the violent act was underway. "After I came to, he held the gun to my temple and said, 'If you move one more time I will kill you.' Then I heard the loudest sound I have ever heard in my entire life: He pulled the hammer of that gun back. From that point on I did not move."

When it was over, she stumbled out of the Jeep and turned back to look once more at her attacker. "He said, 'Thanks for a good time. But whatever you do, don't think you're the first and you certainly won't be the last.' Then he looked at me and said, 'Now, get out of my face.'"

Reesee took off running toward her car. She passed the second guy on the way back. She could hear the girls laughing as she got closer. When she got there, they were fine, though they could plainly see that she had been beaten. Reesee was in shock. She just got in and drove home as fast as her car would take her.

Reesee had an overwhelming feeling of being dirty and defiled, so she took a long shower. She wanted to wash away the act that had violated her body. Then she took the clothes she had been wearing that night and burned them. She wanted anything that was even touching her body during that hideous act to be destroyed.

Soon after the incident, Reesee decided to go to the authorities for help. But when she called a rape crisis line, she learned some hard lessons about her current situation. Without an eyewitness, her case would quickly come down to a "he said, she said" defense. Also, she had no physical proof. Because she had taken a shower and burned her clothes—as so many rape victims do—she had actually made it impossible to prove she had been sexually assaulted.

Reesee wanted to turn to her family. But she felt she couldn't. "It was a very devastating time for my family. In April of 1993, my dad had severe chest pains. By the time he realized what was happening and got to the hospital, he had had a massive heart attack. From April to November, he had six operations where they clean out your arteries with angioplasty. He was fighting desperately for his life. We did not know from one day to the next if he was going to survive.

"My mom had been going through quite a lot trying to stay strong for my sisters and me. She had taken over being the head of the family and the head of the household while Dad was recovering."

Reesee felt totally alone. She feared that if she went to the authorities, something might come out in the hometown paper. Even if she talked to a friend, she was afraid that word might make it back to her family. With her father in such a delicate condition, Reesee felt trapped in a cold prison of silence.

While her face healed from the cuts and bruises from the attack, Reesee lied to her parents: She told them she had the flu and could not come over. Because her dad was in a weakened state, she said, she didn't want to expose him to sickness.

So she stayed away. She didn't talk to those who cared for her the most. She didn't talk to the authorities. And she didn't talk to God. She could not fathom how God would let something as hideous as this happen to her. She was bitter and angry and her silence literally started to kill her.

As if that weren't enough, her attacker began stalking her. "He was leaving cards. He was calling me. I would call the police, but there were no stalking laws at that time. Every time I would turn around, he was there, or there was a card on my doorstep. It didn't matter where I lived. It didn't matter how many times I changed my phone number. He had his ways of finding me. He was threatening me constantly. He told me he was going to finish the job he had started that night."

With no one to talk to and still angry at God, her life started to change dramatically. "Everything I believed in died. Everything I was died. Everything I loved died—except the love of my family. I loved them enough that I kept it from them. I hated God more than anything in the world. I wanted nothing to do with Him. I absolutely refused to listen to anyone talk about Him. I felt that everything I had been taught in church was a lie.

"It was a rough few years for me. I started smoking. I lived a very promiscuous life. I didn't care what I did. All my foundations were gone. I started eating a lot. In the end, I ate myself to a weight of over five hundred pounds. I was on a self-destructive course. I had become someone I didn't like. I became someone I wanted to destroy. I wanted to die."

Finally, Reesee was ready for it all to end. "I was sitting there one day and I decided I had had it. I couldn't take it anymore. There was no God. I was totally unlovable. I felt so alone. I made a will and then sat in front of my TV taking pills. I was going to end it right then and there."

But God was not ready for Reesee's life to end. He spoke to her through a preacher on television. Pat Robertson, host of *The 700 Club,* was on TV at that moment.

"Dr. Robertson looked right at me and said, 'Young lady, stop what you are doing! God does love you. I know you think that He doesn't, but He does. What happened to you should've never happened. Jesus loves you and healing will come. Suicide is not your way out.' I was just blown away. I just knew it was for me."

Reesee prayed and cried for hours that night. Her heart filled with that loving presence that she had known as a little girl. Her life truly started to turn around.

She decided to break her silence and talk to her mom and dad about the rape. "My mom, of course, started crying. My dad looked at me and he said, 'If you think this would make a difference about how we feel about you, you are so wrong. We love you now more than ever. We always have and we always will.'

"We talked for a long time and as we were getting ready to leave my dad said, 'I want you to understand something. At some point you are going to have to forgive him for what he did to you.' I looked at Dad and I said, 'I can't.' And he said, 'I know you can't now, but one day you will.' Then, with tears in his eyes, he said, 'He hurt you and we love you so deeply, so one day your mom and I will have to somehow forgive him, too.'"

And so Reesee's emotional healing began. She started speaking to church groups about the complex issues raised by rape. And her spiritual healing was moving forward, too, but still she could not understand how God had abandoned her in her most desperate hour.

After speaking to a church group, Reesee was approached by a gentle, gray-haired woman. She said something to Reesee that literally changed her whole outlook.

"This little old lady walked up to me and said, 'I want you to know that that's the most inspiring story I've ever heard. But I want to tell you something, and I don't want you to get offended at me.' She said, 'Did you ever think about why you are not dead? That man pulled that hammer back, and he could've easily pulled the trigger. The reason is that God was there and He did protect you.'

"I had never looked at it that way. That was the first time I realized that God had been looking out for me or had an angel there for me, after all. Because that man could've killed me, but he didn't."

Reesee is now a changed woman. She's lost over 330 pounds, and her heart that was once so cold and hard has become a conduit of God's love to others. Her personal relationship with the Lord has grown into a solid, daily walk of prayer and thanksgiving. She has been able to touch hundreds of lives with her message of hope. She often speaks to groups and has been appointed by crisis agencies to help with recent court cases. She serves as an advocate to women and children who have been sexually attacked or abused.

"I realize now that the rape was not my fault. I did not deserve it. I am no longer a victim. I am a survivor. And I will continue to survive it every single day. I will continue fighting for those that can't fight for themselves.

"If it weren't for God I couldn't help the women and children that I do now. The reason I went through what I did was so that I could become a voice for all those women and children who are hurting and don't have the courage to break their silence. That is what I live for. That is why I am here. I thank God that He loved me enough that He did not let me die. He gave the strength and He gave me the wings to fly again."

Paul Tribus

Vietnam Vets:
The Lost Generation

The first night up in the DMZ we were overrun.
I remember throwing grenades. I fired that machine gun.
We had the Vietcong coming up the hill. It was right out war.

When Paul Tribus of Hampton, Virginia, talks to you, you see in his eyes that he's a man of depth and character. Those eyes have seen their share of bloodshed and atrocities—the kind of nightmarish scenes that we hope to never see in our lifetimes. In the turbulent sixties, Paul fought in Vietnam.

"Vietnam was a teenage war. It stole my teenage years. That's why a lot of vets are trying to recapture their youth somehow. I had this instant growing-up experience after graduating high school in 1967. When I should have been in college or running hot rods on the beach, I was in a war."

Like so many vets, Paul suffers from posttraumatic stress syndrome. "It's like a young child who is molested or traumatized, but then as an adult intentionally gets busy. And there's nothing wrong with people doing that, but they don't face their inner trauma."

Paul cites a staggering statistic. "They say that 20 percent of our population today is directly related to a Vietnam vet. And 90 percent of Vietnam combat vets are divorced. I've met guys on their eighth or ninth marriages." It truly is a generation of American men who have lost their way.

His memories of the war are vivid and haunting. "I remember coming off the plane like it was yesterday. It was like opening up an oven door set on six hundred degrees. The first night up in the DMZ we were overrun. I remember throwing grenades. I fired that machine gun. We had the Vietcong coming up the hill. It was right out war. Grenades flying. Bodies flying. People yelling and screaming."

Paul was in combat for 395 days. He says the hardest part of the whole ordeal was that you knew a bullet could come for you at any moment. "You're not safe anywhere. There's no safe place. There was a knot in my stomach for that year that is indescribable. It's such a knot of terror."

If the enemy didn't kill you, the jungle would. "A drill instructor once told us, 'Marines, 99 percent of the snakes in Vietnam are poisonous; the other one percent will swallow you whole.' I had snakes crawl right over my head and body. You just dealt with that. One buddy got bit by a black widow and just about died. That's why they say Marines always sleep with one eye open. You never really got a good night's sleep. How could you?"

Another dark factor of Vietnam was the emotional isolation. Each soldier put up unbreakable walls to survive psychologically. The fighting was so intense that the guy standing beside you one minute could easily be dead the next. "That's why a lot of guys didn't even get close to one another because they didn't want to become buddies. They were afraid to get close to a person because then they get killed and you're throwing them on a chopper."

Our country had never before fought an intricate war like Vietnam. At times you could not tell friend from foe. "In the DMZ, I knew who my enemies were: If they wore a different uniform than me, they were the enemy. But down south around Da Nang you were dealing with villagers. The person cutting your hair during the day could be shooting at you at night. The Vietcong would come in and terrorize them, saying, 'We're going to kill your kids if you don't go out and throw these grenades at the Marines tonight!'"

Conversely, the Vietcong often threatened the children and told them if they did not cooperate, the Vietcong would kill their mothers. "They used children like demolition equipment. They would put a live grenade on a child and have him walk up to a gate. That's why you learned not to trust anybody or anything. You dealt with so much uncertainty. Anything you touched could be a booby trap."

One of the most devastating booby traps was called a pungee pit. The Vietcong dug deep pits in the jungles, then disguised the holes. At the bottom of the pits they would plant spears or knives smeared with dung. The unlucky soldier would not only be injured in the fall and savagely cut by the knives, but his wound would be automatically infected. Many soldiers contracted gangrene from these traps and had to have limbs amputated.

Vietnam was a disgusting war. Paul fought valiantly and was awarded two Purple Hearts for his courage and bravery. He was an exemplary soldier. But for years afterward, hellish images of war haunted his mind.

But in the midst of this horrible war, something happened to Paul that would change the rest of his life. "I was coming off of an R&R leave and going back to rejoin my unit. I was lying outside trying to catch a little nap while I waited for a truck to come by. Along blew this Holy Joe witnessing tract. So I read it. That was the first time I'd ever been shown the message of salvation. So when I read it, it meant something to me." After reading the cartoon story about Holy Joe, Paul prayed and asked Jesus Christ to come into his life.

When his tour of duty was over, Paul got married and later became a pastor. But even with his strong relationship with the Lord, he suffered from posttraumatic stress syndrome. He knew something was wrong but tried to lose himself in his church work to keep his mind off the horrible memories of the war.

Even day-to-day life was challenging for Paul. Certain images, smells, and situations would trigger dark memories. Those memories would trigger his anger, and that unresolved anger would inadvertently turn toward his wife and his children. Other times Paul seemed distant or agitated. While on a leisurely boating outing with his wife, Paul looked transfixed at the tree line along the riverbank. He was back in Vietnam.

Paul knows of a vet who would experience intense anxiety on a certain day every week. His wife complained that every Tuesday he would become unbearably irritable. They finally realized the problem: Tuesday was trash day. The large trash bags that lined his street reminded him of the body bags he'd had to fill with dead soldiers' bodies in Vietnam.

After bottling up his anger for years, Paul heard about a Vietnam vets conference at CBN in Virginia Beach. He decided to go. Through that meeting with other Christian vets and praying with his wife and children, Paul began to heal from years of deep-rooted pain. He has spent the years that followed helping others find the healing he found that day.

Paul feels the first step to full recovery is a clear one. "That first step is having a personal relationship with Christ. You can't clean yourself up. God's got to clean you up. I don't care what kind of filth you're in or how bad you think you are, Christ is your answer."

Paul has served as the state coordinator for Point Man Ministries. He encourages vets to get involved with Point Man or other groups where they can talk about their experiences openly and fully. "Find somebody who has gone through what you've been through or who at least understands and has compassion. And hopefully someone who incorporates God's Word in their advice.

"You don't have to be a victim," Paul says. "But you can have *victory*. I like to break down the word *victory* into two parts. The first part sounds like the word *victim*. The last part sounds like *story*. Many a Vietnam vet has found victory by realizing he is a victim who now has a story to tell. And it can be a good story because it's a story of deliverance. You don't have to be a victim. You can have the victory."

RICK SWEENIE

When No One Came

One time my wife stuck a gun in my hand
in the middle of the night because somebody was trying
to get in through the window.
I came very close to shooting it out with people.

R ick Sweenie of Bellevue, Nebraska, was trapped in the
dark world of drugs and violence and crime. His drug
habit overpowered every thought in his mind. "When
you're addicted, drugs are all you think about," he says. "You
don't think of your family, you don't trust anyone. And of
course you don't think about God. It is complete darkness. It's
like you're alive but you are really dead."

His life was caught in a hellish vortex. The more he used
the drugs, the more he had to use them. It was like a gigantic
boa constrictor wrapping itself firmly around Rick's body,
tightening its grip ever so slowly, squeezing the life out of him.

"After a while I couldn't even catch the thrill of the drugs.

They had complete control of my life. I used drugs every day, all day—as much as my body could take. I had to have drugs even to get out of bed. I couldn't work. I couldn't do anything." The drugs pushed him to the brink of insanity. "Once I went twenty-four hours a day for seven days without food or drink or sleep."

His dark hunger for drugs forced him into a life of drug dealing. He saw no other way to support a five-hundred-dollar-a-day habit. "I was a very prominent drug dealer in the area. I thought I was climbing the ladder of success because I was meeting all the big drug dealers. I was a little frightened at first since everybody carried guns, but it didn't take very long before I was right there with them."

Drugs and firearms went hand in hand. Rick's philosophy was that he was not going to get caught in a gunfight holding only a knife. "I had a lot of guns," he says. "There were situations where I owed money for drugs and the dealers would come to my house after their money. One time my wife stuck a gun in my hand in the middle of the night because somebody was trying to get in through the window. I came very close to shooting it out with people."

During drug-induced rages, Rick would go on shooting sprees around the house, even shooting at his wife and the dog. Later he'd tell his friends what he'd done, and they'd have a good laugh.

His life of drugs and crime landed Rick in jail so many times he cannot remember a specific number. At one point he faced five felony charges. Finally Rick realized he was in trouble.

One night he was alone in his cold, dark cell, evaluating his life. Sitting on his thin mattress, Rick began to look back and remember his childhood. He recalled going to church and Sunday school. He remembered a kind old gentleman that had come to his mother's house one evening to tell Rick about God.

He realized that all through his life there had been people who reached out to tell him about the love of Jesus. For so long Rick had refused to think about God, frightened that people would call him a Jesus freak if he ever turned to religion to help him.

But that lonely night, Rick found much more than religion to help him—he found a relationship. "I just prayed all by myself in that jail cell. I had a repentant heart and was very sorry for all the things I had done. I really believed in what Christ did for me, and I placed my faith and trust in the forgiveness of Jesus. And I was crying."

As the tears rolled down his face that night, Rick knew he was a new man. He knew from that point forward he would be a better husband and a more loving father to his two young children. His hunger for drugs was replaced by a hunger for God.

Rick longed to talk to somebody about his new faith, so he asked the jailer if anyone from local churches ever came by to talk with the inmates. The officer assured him there would be someone coming by, but nobody came. "For seventy-one days I sat in that jail. Not one person from the church ever came by to talk to me. No one came by to give me a Bible. No one came by to give me some prayer time or some counseling or guidance. No one came by."

Ultimately he was moved to another prison. "It was not

until I went to the prison in Iowa where they had a chaplain that I finally got to talk to someone. This chaplain was a man of God. He had volunteers coming into the jail who would minister to the inmates. They would hold our hands. They would pray for our families and encourage us so much."

The times he spent reading his Bible, praying with others, and begging God to restore his life and family reshaped Rick in a miraculous way. It was a long road, and it took him years to break some dark habits, but when people meet Rick today they cannot believe he once lived such a hardened criminal life.

It's been many years since Rick's release from prison, but now he's in jail again—as a prison chaplain. Rick is a regional director for Good News Jail and Prison Ministries. He says he will always remember those dark days when no one came by to see him. It is the memory of those days that drives him to reach out to people without hope. "That's really what our ministry is all about: giving hope to a hopeless man. Before I was arrested, there was no hope. But all of a sudden I was filled with hope through Jesus Christ."

Over the years God has truly restored Rick's life. Instead of a life filled with violence, his life is filled with peace. Rick and his loving wife, Margie, have been married for over thirty-two years now. Their two grown children visit often, bringing over the grandchildren. When they all get together there are no sounds of gunshots and drunkenness, but the gentle sounds of children laughing and playing.

After years of exemplary service as a chaplain, many people rallied to help Rick get a pardon from the governor of Iowa. In a rare move, a total pardon was granted. "Governor Brandstad said these words to me: 'You know that a pardon is like it never happened.' And I thought, God's pardon is like that, too!

"When I prayed in that jail cell and realized that Jesus had been punished for my sins when He died on the cross, I was cleansed through and through. That was the day I received my pardon from God. Though the one from Governor Brandstad is wonderful, the pardon I'm most grateful for is the pardon I received from God."

CHIP GILLETTE

And He Shall Reign Forever and Ever

A strong smell of gunpowder permeated the whole building.
Nine-millimeter shell casings littered the floor....
Then they saw one of the gunman's first victims.

On September 15, 1999, the unthinkable happened at Wedgwood Baptist Church in Fort Worth, Texas. On that fateful Wednesday night, a lone gunman entered the church building and killed seven people.

Imagine going to your church, the one place where you always feel safe and loved. Imagine you've gone to a Christian concert that night with your closest friends. Now imagine that not all of you will make it out of the church alive.

I can't think of a more frightening scene than what the five hundred or so young people experienced that night. When it was all over, three young adults, four high school students, and the gunman were dead. Our hearts broke for each of their families and for all the lives that were tragically altered that horrible night.

Chip Gillette is an active member of Wedgwood Baptist. He's been a Sunday school teacher and a deacon. His wife is the pastor's secretary and the church receptionist. His children have played an active role in the church's youth group. Their home is right across the street—only 150 feet from the church.

Chip is also a police officer. He was the first officer on the scene that Wednesday night.

Chip remembers the evening started out so normally. It was around 6:20. The Christian band Forty Days was performing a youth concert at the church. Chip's daughter was there. Since Chip was working the midnight shift that evening, he was at home trying to rest up before going to work. He was stretched out on the couch in the den. The TV was on in the background. Everyone else had gone over to the church.

In the Bible, Balaam is warned of great danger by his donkey. In much the same way, Chip was warned by their family dog.

"Jake, our yellow Labrador, went crazy. He ran to the front room and barked. He just kept barking and barking. I hadn't heard anybody ring the doorbell. I thought maybe I'd dozed off."

Chip went to the front room to investigate. He saw that Jake was extremely agitated. "The thing that really struck me was the fact that all the hair on his back was standing up like a ridge. He'd done that in the past, but not to this extreme. Even the very thin hairs close to his nose were standing up on end. And all the way down his tail his hair was standing on end. He was up on the hope chest in front of the bay window. He had his nose to the curtain looking out the glass and was still barking."

Chip peered through the window but didn't see anything that should be making the dog upset. He was about to yell at Jake and force him down from the window. But the dog's continued fierce intensity prompted Chip to take a second look. This time something caught his eye.

"I saw two men come out from around the western side of the church. They were looking up and down the street and back up at the church building. I thought it was kind of strange. When you're a police officer you think everything is strange. I figured I'd better go outside and see what was going on."

When he came out of his house, one of the deacons ran to him from the church, frantically yelling that people had been shot. "It was just like a complete shadow came over me," Chip says. "I can't even explain the feeling. It was just like all of the blood had run out of my body."

Chip sprang into action. "I ran back into the house. The first thing I did was grab my police radio. When I was able to get through, I just said, 'Wedgwood Baptist Church, 5522 Whitman Avenue. There's shooting inside the church. Send everything you've got.' And I threw the radio on the bed."

He grabbed his pistol, threw on his police vest and shirt so no one would mistake him for the shooter, and bolted out the front door. As he dashed across the street, a police car screeched to a halt in front of the church. "I flagged him down and he drove right up to me. Together we went in the same glass door the shooter had gone in."

Chip says the scene was indescribable. "A strong smell of

gunpowder permeated the whole building. Nine-millimeter shell casings littered the floor. It looked like someone had come in there and emptied two or three magazines of nine-millimeter ammunition everywhere." Then they saw one of the gunman's first victims. "There was blood all over her and even draining down onto the floor off the sofa that she was lying on."

They moved toward the sanctuary but still weren't sure what was going on. A failed robbery, perhaps? A gang-related incident? They weren't sure how many gunmen were in the sanctuary. Over the other officer's radio, Chip heard that a SWAT team was on the way. That was good, but he knew it could take up to two hours for them to arrive. Foremost in his mind was the knowledge that his daughter was in there. No matter how dangerous it was, he was getting into that sanctuary now!

Chip and the other officer split up to enter the sanctuary through different doors. "The shooting was still going on. When I got to the door I just threw the door open. I heard one more gunshot as I entered."

After the last gunshot, there was a dramatic pause. Finally someone yelled, "He's shot himself. Let's get out of here!"

Hundreds of young people began to come out from under the pews and run for the exits. "I pushed through the sea of people and got to the back of the sanctuary. I was face-to-face with the shooter. He was still sitting upright. I was looking at him and he was looking at me. I was just waiting for him to make his move. He was seated in a pew that was up against the back wall."

Within seconds, the gunman's eyes became vacant and his body went limp. "He fell over to his left side. I saw the small wound on the one side of his head and then the large amount of blood he was losing on the other side. He was making a gurgling sound. It was obvious he was incapacitated."

Once the gunman was dead, Chip looked around in disbelief. Though he is a veteran of over two hundred homicide scenes, nevertheless he was stunned to see this kind of bloodshed in his own church.

"It was unbelievable. There were just literally rivers of blood running from the wounded and dead at the back and running down the aisles and pooling at the front of the church. Up and down the hallway there were shoes—people had literally run out of their shoes to get out of the building."

By this time, police from all over the city had begun to converge on the little church. Chip made his way outside.

"Out in the hallway there were three bodies, and inside the worship center there were four more, plus the shooter. Then there were several who had been injured. Some were still lying around waiting for medical attention."

Chip was soon reunited with his daughter and his wife, who were both unhurt.

The tragedy at Wedgwood stunned the state of Texas and the nation. It has caused many to wonder where God was. Here was a man shooting Christians in a church sanctuary—surely a loving God would've intervened. Where was God?

Chip sums up his feelings on the strange presence he felt that night. "When I first went in through the glass doors, it felt like I was walking into the midst of hell. I felt the very presence of evil. But on top of that I also felt the presence of God. It was like evil was trying to come into the holy of holies. There was a spiritual battle going on.

"The tragic part is that eight people lost their lives. There are those who were injured and many who are still suffering because of their injuries. Many families will continue to suffer because of their loss. But God has given the victory even in the midst of all of this."

No one would say that what happened wasn't horrible. However, many feel the losses that night could've been much greater. This man was on a mission to kill as many people as possible, but though he shot sixty-eight rounds of ammunition, only eight lives were lost. The police found another ninety rounds of ammunition that he didn't even use.

He threw a pipe bomb into the front of the sanctuary. It could've easily killed or injured forty to fifty more young people. The damage, however, was amazingly minimal. "When it exploded, it just sent all the shrapnel straight up into the sky, up into the ceiling and part of it into the wall," Chip says. "It didn't injure anybody."

Some believe the biggest miracle that night was the fact that the children initially thought it was a skit. Earlier that evening the youth pastor had informed the kids that there would be a special surprise skit that night. When the gunman started shooting, some high schoolers literally thought they were seeing paintballs flying through the air.

"If people had panicked and run for the doors it would've given this man targets to shoot at. Instead of having seven funerals we could've easily had a hundred and fifty to two hundred. As it was they stayed down in the pews. Even though they giggled and laughed at him and thought it was all a joke, for the most part no one panicked and ran for the doors. He had nothing to shoot at."

Chip told the media that one of the biggest heroes of the evening was Jake. If his dog had not been persistent in getting his attention, Chip says he may never have looked out the window and made that crucial police radio call. The national media was astonished at the police response time. The time the first call went in to the police to the time the last victim was at the hospital spanned an amazing twenty-eight minutes. These crucial life-saving minutes helped others who were severely injured.

Acts of sympathy and kindness poured in from all over the nation. Cards, letters, and e-mails flooded the church. A large paper banner filled with personal notes of encouragement from Columbine High School students was hung in the church lobby. Churches of many different denominations expressed deep sympathy and support. One church even came on the property to pray for the healing of those who had been broken by the tragedy.

After the shooting, Chip felt the Lord urging him to go into the sanctuary and look for something. He had no idea what this might be. The police investigators had thoroughly mapped every bullet and scoured the crime scene for evidence. But as Chip moved through the worship center he felt drawn to a particular spot. When he looked, he found something the crime scene investigators had missed.

"I could see where a bullet had gone through the side of the pew and then gone into a hymnal rack. I found a hymnal sitting at an odd angle, so I picked it up."

A chill went down Chip's spine. When he touched the hymnal he felt a bulge. He sat down in the pew and opened the damaged book. Inside, he found a bullet. The heat of the bullet had literally fused many pages of the hymnal together. The book's broken spine made the hymnal fall open to a specific song—"The Hallelujah Chorus."

"It just fell open to that hymn and that's where that bullet was lodged in such a perfect way. The tip of the bullet was pointed at that part of the chorus where it says, 'King of kings, Lord of lords, and He will reign forever and ever.' That was what God had wanted me to find."

The Sunday immediately following the shooting, the congregation of Wedgwood Baptist held their regular worship service. "It was almost like being in heaven with God Himself," Chip says. "It was unbelievable. There was an overpowering presence and a sense of joy and peace that God had given."

As news spread of what had happened at Wedgwood Baptist Church that fateful day in September, hundreds if not thousands of people have come to the Lord. What Satan meant for evil, God meant for good.

Chip states it this way: "God is in control even in the midst of terror. God has His hand in it. Even when it looks like evil has triumphed, even in the midst of turmoil, God holds us in His hand. No matter what evil may come upon us, He is King of kings and Lord of lords—and He will reign forever."

Conclusion

Now that you have read these amazing stories, I hope you are encouraged in your own life. I pray you have a newfound hope to face the future.

In all these stories, no matter what people were going through, no matter what situations they found themselves in, they still felt God's care in their lives.

For Paul Tribus it came in the form of a small, gentle breeze that blew a gospel tract in his direction. For Cornel Potra it was God silencing the beep from his wristwatch alarm. And for Denise Jones it was her son opening his eyes just a little bitty slit. David Holden felt the overpowering presence of God, while invisible arms in the midst of a giant twister sheltered Marilyn Burleigh and her children.

God gives each of us some stories like the stories in this book. Maybe not so dramatic, but tales just as compelling that prove His nearness in moments of crisis or loss. I challenge you to look back on your stories with joy. Build a memorial of your own to remind you of God's everlasting love. And then point out these markers to your family and friends and neighbors. Perhaps they need encouragement, too.

Tell them that no matter how hard our lives may be, how dark the circumstances may seem, how violent the storms of life may be swirling around, God is in control. He is always with us, protecting and loving and guiding in the midst of life's storms. He truly holds us in the hollow of His hand.

Printed in the United States
by Baker & Taylor Publisher Services